# EVERY DAY'S
# A GOOD DAY

# EVERY DAY'S A GOOD DAY

Terry **Gordon**

# EVERY DAY'S A GOOD DAY

iUniverse books may be ordered through booksellers or by contacting:

iUniverse
1663 Liberty Drive
Bloomington, IN 47403
www.iuniverse.com
1-800-Authors (1-800-288-4677)

ISBN: 978-1-4917-8473-0 (sc)
ISBN: 978-1-4917-8474-7 (e)

Library of Congress Control Number: 2015921490

Print information available on the last page.

iUniverse rev. date: 06/02/2016

# DEDICATION

This book is dedicated to my sister Dorothy, without whose guidance, understanding, trust, honesty, encouragement, love, passion and non-judgmental character—I can in all honesty and without hesitation say—this book would not have been possible. Whether I was chatting with her by phone on my way home after a long day at the office, spending time with her on weekends at the trailer near Port Perry or visiting her home in Stouffville and then Oshawa, the end result would  always be the same. She would make my bad day a good day or my good day a better day.

Unfortunately, Dorothy passed away in October 2013 and now joins her family, along with our brothers (Edward, Henry and George) and sister (Vera). I miss them all so much. Dorothy's influence on what I do today is still very much present. When I have a difficult decision to make, all I have to do is close my eyes and ask myself, "What would my big sister want me to do?" I know that whatever decision is made, right or wrong, I will have her approval. She will always have my back.

Dorothy, I still miss you very much. Whenever I am about to enter my home, I am reassured of your presence because I lovingly look down and see the weathered fisherman and his dog—your gift to me—right outside my door. It's at that very moment that I know that not only is my house now a home; it gives me the reassurance that you are still watching over me and that everything is going to be okay.

I love you!

Your baby brother, Terry

# CONTENTS

Acknowledgments ....................................................... ix

1   The Reasons Why ................................................... 1

2   Thoughts to Ponder ............................................. 15

3   Thoughts to Ponder (on the Lighter Side) ......................... 181

4   Final Thoughts ................................................. 273

# ACKNOWLEDGMENTS

I must pay tribute and give heartfelt thanks to the following people not only for their help in putting this project together with their talents but also for their support, enthusiasm and words of encouragement in making it a reality.

## Danko Opsenica

Danko is not just a co-worker with a great sense of humour; he's an integral part of our engineering team working with computers and drawings. Up until recently, I had no idea of his artistic side. I was overwhelmed and speechless (which does not happen often) in the face of his God-given talent in the art of cartooning. I am humbled yet at the same time excited to see Danko's artistic flair—which I could only dream of—put on paper for humorous purposes. Pure genius!

## Jennifer Gordon

I may be a little biased as her father, but ever since Jennifer was able to hold a crayon, a pencil or a brush, it was quite evident that there was an up-and-coming artist among us. She has a gift for creating something special with her hands that others can only imagine. Top that off with her passion, and there is no end to her creativity. Her recent graduation from OCAD University is a testament to her artistic talent, as that program is very demanding—but as usual Jennifer came through with flying colours (no pun intended). It never ceases to amaze me what she can create, and the sketches she came up with here are no exception. I have always been a proud father of all my children, and Jennifer makes me more proud each and every day.

## Nancy Zurba

I have known Nancy for approximately a dozen years now and describe her as a well-respected business professional with a positive outlook on life and a great sense of humour. When I first mentioned to her my dilemma in finding a suitable person to not only decipher my chicken scratch but also organize it in Microsoft Word, I was pleasantly surprised when Nancy stepped up and said she would like to do it. She has been nothing short of a positive inspiration throughout the entire process. I really should not be surprised, because after all, it is Nancy I'm talking about.

## Marybel Unabia

I must give a heartfelt thank you to Marybel for whom has been an angel sent from above. She has had such a positive influence on me from day one. From her contagious work ethics to her patient, kind, caring, forgiving and understanding personality of which are second to none. Everything she does comes from her heart, and without looking for recognition. Without hesitation I can honestly say that she has opened my eyes to once again enjoy life and has helped me to achieve goals that I never thought were possible. Although never taken for granted, there are times when I should show a little more appreciation.

# 1

# THE REASONS WHY

Here at the beginning of this book, I'd like to just briefly touch upon my challenges while growing up. Keeping everything bottled up has taken a toll on me both physically and psychologically. It was in 1999 that I finally sat down and started writing in great detail about all of the challenges and unanswered questions, trying to piece together the past so I could make sense of it all.

I relived many unhappy moments while writing and at times broke down in tears as I sought some sort of explanation. Many questions were left unanswered, but I had to ask them before I could start the healing process. I devoted 57 pages of writing—including sketches, clippings and photographs—to try to piece together and sort out my past. I went directly to the heart of my challenges and noted what I did to conquer my demons. I wrote of how I survived my biggest ordeal—not with anger, resentment, guilt or sympathy but with reasoning, thought, understanding and compassion. I wrote it all down not for others but for myself.

These writings were shared with only a select few because of the trust, respect and love I have for them. I know they understand where I'm coming from and the ordeals I have been put through. There have been enough tears shed in private to last more than a lifetime, but at present I am finding peace in my life—a little more every day.

I have no idea why it took me so long to get started with this, my second book. I have wanted to do it for quite some time, and if I'm not mistaken, the idea came to me a little over four years ago when I was feeling down in the dumps. Anyone who knows me will tell you that I can procrastinate with the best of them. It's a trait that has been evident ever since I was separated in 1999. At the time, I had lost interest in the simple things and had no cares or concerns for anything. I could not even care for my own well-being.

There were times when I would go into my own little bubble world and not speak to anyone, not say hello to passers-by, not smile when someone said good morning in my direction, not enjoy a sunny day in the summertime, not enjoy children laughing while they played—you get the idea of how miserable I had become. It felt like I had gone from a quiet, outgoing, self-confident, happy person to a sarcastic, reserved, insecure, miserable person with a gigantic chip on my shoulder.

To be painfully honest, I felt that the world had screwed me over royally by leaving me on my own once again. I have a handwritten portion of what I wrote back in 1999 after my separation, which literally tore my world apart. There was so much I didn't understand or remember. That's why some things were left blank; to this day, there are some answers that are not clear to me, or my memory has either failed me or just blocked out the past.

I have not included my handwritten thoughts right after separation, because there are too many unknowns. Even after soul-searching and painstaking sleepless nights trying to figure things out, there are still blanks, and I have left them as blanks. Maybe someday I can fill them in. I really have this fear of being alone. It scares the hell out of me.

The separation was strike two in my life. Strike one was when my mother passed away. Without any prior warning of how sick she was, and without even a chance to see her or say goodbye, I lost my mother to cancer in October 1964, approximately two months after my 12th birthday. Very shortly after that, my father moved in with another woman and her two teenage children. About two years after that, he decided he wanted to continue his life up north with this woman—with, I might add, no explanation as to why or of any options I might have had. There was no way for me to stay with him except to go to Wasaga Beach to become part of a rural community, and that was not what I had in mind. I had my own vision of what I wanted to do with my life, my future and my dreams.

That meant being on my own and fending for myself before I turned 14. If my sister Vera hadn't intervened and taken me in for a while, this would have put me over the edge. I was unstable at the best of times, and for those who knew me—whether as a classmate, fellow part-time worker (I had three part-time jobs while putting myself through high school), hockey teammate or neighbour—there was a mask that concealed my true feelings. I could do this so convincingly that I actually fooled myself on occasion into thinking I was a happy person.

Maybe that's why, for as long as I can remember, I have found it so difficult to open up to anyone. After my mother's sudden death, I became a loner, devoid of happiness and peace of mind. My only way of dealing with any situation was some sort of anger—unleashing sarcasm, throwing things against the wall, putting a fist through a sheet of drywall, banging my head against a wall or destroying comic books, cards and pictures. I might refuse to eat for days or take long drives to nowhere in my later years. The only good thing that can be said of the outbursts was that the only possessions broken or destroyed were my own. A small consolation for these unacceptable, childish acts, but I have learned to look on the bright side of everything, regardless of how miniscule it may be. I'll bet there is still room for improvement.

I must admit to one instance that I am extremely ashamed to have in my repertoire. If it had happened recently, there could have been criminal charges filed and maybe a little jail time. As everyone who watches hockey knows, dirty hits (especially to the head) can bring charges if a player is seriously injured. I guess I was approaching my 17th birthday when the game I was playing in got a little out of hand. I was the goaltender, and I was tired of being slashed at the back of my leg where there was no padding. I decided to take the matter into my own hands—or, in fact, a goal stick, which was my weapon of choice.

As the play went up ice, I raised my stick feverishly over my head. As the player turned around and was about to skate back up the ice, I came down so hard on the back of his helmet that it cracked. I saw him fall down face first on the ice, and then blood started to ooze out from the crack in his helmet. He was not moving at all. It was at that moment that I realized the anger inside me was out of control. It was an unacceptable way of dealing with my issues, and I had to take responsibility for what I had done. Boy, did I ever, to the tune of a 10-game suspension. That really hurt—although my only real concern was for the person I'd almost beheaded earlier.

It was time to do something about all this built-up anger, but where would I go—and, more importantly, who would I talk to? Back in the mid-sixties, there was not much in the line of help. Hell, I couldn't even get direction from the guidance department at my high school. The only thing they did for me was give me a job to make a few extra dollars to help me support myself. That was in Grade 9.

On top of working at Maple Leaf baseball stadium at the bottom of Bathurst Street during baseball season for the AAA organization (better known as the minors; this was also where the infamous Sparky Anderson started his coaching career) as the one who sells pop, popcorn, peanuts, ice cream and other items, I was also employed at Maple Leaf Gardens on Carlton Street during hockey season doing the same. I was there the last time the Leaf won the Stanley Cup, and that was in 1967. Now, on top of the two jobs I already had, I was hired by the TTC to work at the Bay and Dundas terminal as a redcap—mostly on the weekends, but if a shift was available, I always picked it up. I needed the funds to pay for my room in a rooming house and for the necessities of survival, like food and clothing. I guess that is where I learned to be self-sufficient. Come to think of it, I really did not have much of a choice. It was sink or swim.

From 1964 to 1970, everything that could go wrong did go wrong to screw up my childhood, adolescence, high school romance and a healthy, loving, compassionate marriage. I really could not get used to being around anyone and creating a relationship. I could not trust anyone with my personal problems. I could not and did not ask anyone for help, as I really believed I could not trust or put my faith in anyone. I had been taken advantage of for most of my life, and to share my feelings and concerns with others was not even a consideration.

The only person I ever put my trust in was my mother, and she was taken from me before I knew what questions I had to ask her as a child growing up looking for guidance. My father was never a choice, as he was hardly there—and when he was, he was intoxicated. Many times he did not come home. So I kept everything inside and put on a hell of an act. Eventually it caught up with me and destroyed any chance of a happy and healthy life during my early years.

It must also be noted that I had good reason for my anger and hatred towards others. Without going into painstaking detail, I'll tell you in short form the following parts of my life—the parts that led me to being who I was—and what I had to do in order to just to get by. I will not mention names; what has been done is now in the past, and there is no intent to bring back and ignite any hatred towards these people. They know who they are, and whether or not they want to acknowledge their acts back then, I really don't care anymore. I am not the one who has to close my eyes at night and relive the nightmares and feel the guilt over what they did.

The following is a brief list of what I have experienced, with the majority happening before I turned 18. They are not in any specific order; I have jotted them down as they came to mind.

- Sexually abused when I was 6—by a dentist or a doctor, I do not recall. I've tried but do not know which one was the good doctor and which one was the bad doctor.
- Constantly ridiculed by groups of students on many occasions, including being surrounded and urinated on many times on my way to and from school.
- Almost drowned while attending a public school outing in Scarborough in Grade 7. When my dad came home, he was very angry that I had embarrassed him. He had no compassion for my ordeal.
- Deprived of my mother just after I turned 12, with no explanation as to how sick she was and no opportunity to say goodbye and tell her I could not go through with what she had asked me to do for her, and that was becoming a priest.
- Sexually harassed/propositioned by men and women who lived in the area when I left work late at night at the Bay and Dundas bus terminal and across the road towards the Ford Hotel, as part of my job was to carry luggage for passengers from the terminal to the hotel. The hotel does not exist today.
- Constantly exposed to alcohol abuse and what it can do to both the individual and the families it destroys. Along with that was the smoking ordeal I'll mention only because, along

with alcohol, it had a hand in the deaths of my mother; my brothers, Henry, Edward (did not drink to my knowledge) and George; my sister Vera; and recently Dorothy, my last sibling (although she had a long and healthy life). She was taken from me in October 2013. I so much wanted this book to be completed before her death, but procrastination is victorious again.

- Sexually abused over a period of about a year and a half while I was close to twelve through fourteen years of age.
- Drugged and raped just before I turned fourteen.
- Constantly thinking about taking my own life while walking along the train tracks at Main Street and Danforth Avenue in my teens.
- Having no one in attendance when personal achievements were presented, including honours all during high school. I played hockey with no one in the stands cheering; I won bowling tournaments with no applauding or looking at the trophies I had just received. Not having a parent present at any good personal event or even at not-so-good events was very hard to accept, especially with all the other parents around me celebrating with their children. I also had to go to all events by myself and travel home by myself. Let me remind you that I was a goaltender while playing hockey and had to carry all the equipment with me on transit. I was maybe 110, 115 pounds soaking wet. Most of my hockey was played at Ted Reeve Arena, at local outdoor rinks or after school. That meant spending half a day sometimes travelling by bus, streetcar, subway and even walking. That was painstakingly hard and tiring and very lonely, to say the least.
- Travelling the Bloor/Danforth subway at night so as not be at the rooming house too early and be forced to listen to all the nonsense that went on between other people in the house. There were times when I completed homework assignments in parks or under a bridge (near Main and Danforth) so I would have peace and quiet to do them. I can even remember falling asleep under bridges, going to school wearing the same clothes and having no lunch.

- Living on my own in Toronto since around fourteen, which meant going home at night to a room in a house in the Beaches area, which at times was home to drunks, drug addicts and prostitutes. Many a night I went to sleep crying.
- Being seduced by two older women on two separate occasions, not knowing what the hell I was doing and feeling guilty afterwards.
- Spending two to three months alone after my left leg was badly injured at the knee. I became best friends with my brace, nicknamed "Casty," and endured a lot of rehab all on my own. That injury basically ended any chance of a hockey career. Depression and anger really escalated after that setback. My dream had been to make it to the NHL. That was the dream of most kids at that time who either played the game on ice or on the street with a ball instead of a puck. Mind you, my lack of size and lack of skill would not have allowed me go too far, but I liked to believe otherwise—my heart and determination were huge. I guess I will never know.
- Travelling all day on the TTC to get to my sister's place for what was supposed a celebration of Christmas, only to find my sister and her husband passed out from drinking. I left immediately and cried while waiting for the Cliffside bus to take me back to the subway so I could make my way back to the rooming house. From that time on, I spent most of the so-called happy family celebrations alone. At least I had no letdowns, as I never showed up to allow them to happen.
- Being introduced by my father as the "mistake child" who wasn't planned—when he bothered to acknowledge me at all.
- Moving every year or two—when my mother was alive, that is—and I don't mean in the same neighbourhood, where I could at least go to the same school and keep a few friends. We would move from the Beaches area to Scarborough, for example, where everything and everyone changed. I could not even have a friend I could confide in and tell things to without judgment or humiliation or sarcasm or finger wagging. That could have been a contributing factor to my code of silence, by which I never shared my problems,

dilemmas, questions, curiosities, needs or happy times. The kind of friend who would want to hear them just did not exist for me.

- Knowing full well that somewhere between here (Toronto) and there (Detroit), I have a set of twin girls who would be around forty-four years old at the time of this writing. I fathered them during a brief relationship with an 18-year-old girl back in 1970 while she was staying in Toronto for her university education. It was a silly and careless thing to do, but I was willing to take full responsibility for my actions. However, she left town with no message for me as to where she was going, no phone number, no answer as to why this was happening, not even a goodbye. I was totally devastated and unsure of what to do. After nearly a decade of searching for answers and trying to contact her and the children, I ran into enough roadblocks to realize that it just wasn't meant to be—plus the resources were not there for me to continue.

- Constantly hearing conflicting stories on who was who in the family, and being told that my last name should not be Gordon because I was a horse of a different colour, as the expression goes. At the time, I even wondered who my father was—or who my mother was, for that matter. There is a dark secret in my family that was never opened up to me, for reasons I will never know. My real last name might be Turnbull (unsure of the spelling), not Gordon. It has never been explained to me by any of my siblings, and now that I have not one sibling left out of five, I guess I will never know. I know that my brother Edward (God rest his soul) was empathetic that my name was Gordon and always would be Gordon; he got very angry whenever it was questioned or brought up by his wife, Nora. I really don't care anymore, but at the time I was just a child, and is it any wonder I had symptoms of insecurity, confusion and anger? I guess that is something else to take to the grave with me.

With all of these of incidents—and I'm sure there are more I've forgotten because of the time frame or because they're so horrendous I've totally blocked them out of my mind as ever happening—is it any wonder that I feel I never had a happy childhood or even experienced adolescence at all? Since nothing was ever done on my behalf, I have kept most of these dark secrets to myself. They cost me my marriage of 24 years—and to my children, Jason, Nicholas, Andrew and Jennifer, all I can say sincerely to each and every one of you is that I am sorry it didn't work out the way it should have or the way I would have liked it to. I would also like to make it very clear that it wasn't for the lack of love for the four of you, as I put everything into being the best father I could be for you, the father you deserved. Obviously I have made some mistakes, and for those I am sorry. I truly love all of you and hope I can be forgiven for my part in the failure of the happy family I had hoped for and I am sure you hoped for as well.

To those close to me, I would like to say that when this feeling arises, it seems like people want to distance themselves from me—and who can blame them? After all, life is supposed to be a happy, wonderful, exciting experience full of love and joy, so why would anyone want to be around someone who is the opposite? To them I would like to share a saying that I read during one of my journeys: "When you least deserve a hug or a bit of love is when you need it most." I hope they might think of its meaning before making judgments.

Depression is becoming more prominent and open in the world today, and it seems that society has finally recognized it as a disease that needs to be attended to both financially and with tons of support. It affects a lot more people than one would think. Names that come to mind include Heath Ledger and Robin Williams—and both of those trained, talented people are gone because of it. Michael Landsberg of TSN openly talks of it, and Clara Hughes is helping with awareness in a big way, as she has had personal issues with it. I guess what I am trying to say is that I am in good company.

Since I never learned how to express my feelings or deal with certain issues of importance—and even when I wanted to talk about them, there was nobody around—I started writing them down on paper. To be quite honest, this actually saved my life one time when I was about thirteen. I was thinking of ending it all by jumping in front of a train while living in the Main and Danforth area on the east end of Toronto. The trains were there a long time before the condos were built, and it was just a wide-open area for anyone to visit and think. I had my notebook (the kind with pencil and paper, not a computer) with schoolwork inside, and for some reason I decided to write my issues down on paper. Ultimately, I convinced myself to not succumb to the stupidity of ending my life. I probably would have chickened out anyway, but you never know when someone is not thinking rationally.

It's really reassuring to know that there is all kinds of help out there today so no one has to deal with loneliness, despair, depression, anxiety, anger and addiction alone. There are call centers, books, courses, anger management classes, psychiatrists, doctors, counsellors, computer help and hospitals—not to mention resources that parents can use to help with their children's problems/issues when they arise, or even better be prepared to actually fix a problem before it starts to be an issue. I just wish that there was something like that around when I needed it. I may not have had certain issues growing up, but again, one never knows.

Finally, we come to the real reason I'm writing a book at this time. Not only am I trying to show my children what I went through growing up (not to make excuses for my end of the problems) and what I had to do to survive; I'd also like to share with them—and hopefully others—some ways to get by when you're not feeling up to par or something is really bothering you. Along the way, I would like to thank a few people who have become so important to me in my life. Some I have known for over forty years. They mean more to me than family, and before this book is complete, everyone will know who they are. There are others I have met over the years whose names I don't know, but I know them by their smile, their way of saying hello and their way of making me feel welcome.

Regardless of the interaction—a friendly greeting as I get my wake-up coffee and muffin at the McDonald's just around the corner from my office in Bolton, dining at Tandori Time in Toronto, having a few laughs with my friends neighbor Massimo, a chat with Joe and Dora at the best flower store around in Woodbridge, a few words of wisdom shared with Zoran when I visit my personal bank in Brampton, pleasantries exchanged with Jenny and the entire staff at Hallmark in Woodbridge while picking out my specialty cards for every occasion, a discussion of my little investments with Nancy (love her happy faces)—I always know that these people will do something to brighten my day. It's always refreshing and rewarding to receive a helpful gesture, a sincere smile or a welcoming hello. Before I finish this book, I hope to acknowledge all those who have made my life a lot better just by being themselves and making me feel welcome. For that, all I can say is thank you from the bottom of my heart.

I would like to explain why I have chosen this alphabetical format, but those who know me well enough will understand how organized I can be. Quite a few years ago, I started to jot down words and observations; ultimately, I saved those items that made a difference in my outlook on life and, more importantly, made me feel a little better about myself and my situation at the time. They helped me cope with my difficulties and began putting a positive sign in my head. I wanted to share them not only with my family and friends but also with those who may be in a similar situation and unable to open up to anyone.

What I propose to do is enlighten those who read about my lifetime of ups and downs and show that there is always a way to smile no matter what you're trying to deal with. No matter how miniscule the bright side may seem, it will be there. Sometimes it is right under your nose, and you just can't see it. I know because there have been numerous times I have refused to see the positive possibilities or hear the right words or recognize any signs that my day could be better. I guess it comes with maturity. But I haven't grown up totally yet, as I have been told many times. One of the few things I learned from my father (he was hardly there for me at all, as I can remember) is to "always keep a bit of a child in you." He also advised us to "wake up every day and thank the Lord for one more day."

To be honest, I truly think there have been times when I carried that first saying a little bit too far. It should be mentioned, before I forget, that although I still have my faults to correct, I have never hurt anyone through those faults—physically, emotionally or financially.

What I have done for this book is methodically accumulate the everyday sights and sounds that have made my outlook on life a brighter one and put them in alphabetical order so I can remember where to look. I have added a little reflection to each of these small discoveries. That is where I will expose not only the important and understanding people who have been there for me and continue to help me today but also those who in my mind, right or wrong, have made my life miserable in the past and continue to jeopardize my sanity.

I have managed to find at least one little story per letter of the alphabet to help my family and close friends understand what I am trying to express and how these things have affected me in a positive manner. If they know me just a little bit, they will get the picture of what is written, why it is written the way it is and how it helps me on a daily basis. Unfortunately, only a handful of very special people may understand why, and that's okay with me. All the rest of my readers, I hope, will be able to paint a picture of how it can help them in one way or another.

If I can put a smile on a stranger's face, make someone laugh at what was written or help just one person feel more positive about life, then I will be a happy camper. But to reiterate, I am primarily doing this for the most important people in my life. I will make known to the world just how important they are to me, the impact they have had on my life and how they have influenced me in a positive manner. By the end of this book, let's see if I can do these very important people justice. If I have, it should be easy to tell who they are and what they mean to me. They will be acknowledged with a few words at the end in a spot all their own.

I would like to end with a poem by Emily Dickinson that I came across many years ago. I periodically recite it to myself when I am alone and feeling sad. It goes as follows:

My life closed twice before its close;
It yet remains to see
if immortality unveil
a third event to me.
So huge, so hopeless to conceive,
as these that twice befell.
Parting is all we know of heaven,
and all we need of Hell.

I hope that there are a few words of wisdom here to help you live every day in a positive manner and get through tough situations or not-so-happy moments. I know these help me, and I find more signs all the time. Thank you, and I hope you enjoy this, even just a little.

# 2
# THOUGHTS TO PONDER

# A

Acknowledge a Good Deed
Always Give
Attitude Change

# Acknowledge a Good Deed

We often forget about the little things in life people do that make a difference. It doesn't have to be a big-ticket item to get acknowledged. It's always nice to hear a compliment about something we've done quietly, without announcing it to the world.

Every time I hear young children or teenagers say thank you when I hold a door open to enter a shopping mall, I let them know how nice it was to hear that, especially when their parents are with them. I get a kick out of it. Similarly, when a person opens a door for me, it could be (in their minds) a way respect the elderly—or, as my kids say, an "old fart." Nevertheless, I will acknowledge the simple but meaningful gesture.

Our children do not get enough compliments or praise. Some parents only show signs of appreciation when their child does something that inflates their ego—something they can brag about. But children need to receive positive reinforcement or encouragement constantly, especially when they think no one is watching.

That's true in the work world as well. Although I have many faults that I constantly have to correct, I try to regularly say things like "thank you," "good job," "you are welcome" or "I have faith in you." I use that last line when someone in our golf group—whether it's Kiran, Nam, Massimo or Yasu—goes for a difficult putt in order to obtain a birdie or par, which in our case is very rare.

# Always Give

If you really want to make your day better, try something that always makes me feel good, and that is giving to others without any justification, thought or expectation. It doesn't have to be a monetary gift, either. Just give someone a smile, or buy someone who works hard a coffee. There's no rhyme or reason to it, just do it, on the spur of the moment.

It doesn't have to be a birthday or Christmas. You don't want to make the recipient feel guilty or cheap for not giving you anything in return. Personally, I would prefer to receive absolutely nothing in return other than a smile, a heartfelt thank you or a warm and meaningful hug.

When special occasions come along, my daughter makes me hand-drawn cards that I cherish. That's all I need. Those mean more to me than anything store-bought she could give to me.

I tell my children that they work hard for their money, so they shouldn't spend it on gifts for me. If I want something special, I have the means and good fortune to buy my own toys. I am rich because of those memories I have engraved in my mind. They don't cost a cent, and believe it or not, those gifts are priceless.

While we're talking about giving, I recommend supporting charities like the Boy Scouts, Air Cadets, Salvation Army or your local fundraising groups. It's just a few coins to you, but the coins add up to some serious money for those groups, and they put it to good use.

# Attitude Change

People can be easily influenced, and there's a tendency to base one's own opinion about an individual, company or organization on a handful of outside opinions or even one individual's opinion. Without first-hand knowledge, however, you could have a misguided interpretation of what to expect lodged in your mind before you actually go find out for yourself.

You should not believe everything you hear, whether it be from a friend, a family member, a newspaper or a co-worker. Don't get me wrong—you should always listen to and respect others' opinions. Ultimately, though, you should draw your own conclusions.

Just because someone, for example, claims that another individual is a bad apple doesn't mean that person *is* a bad apple. You must consider the source and then make your own decision after careful thought and deliberation. An attitude without proper justification is neither warranted nor fair to that person. Those with brash opinions should stop and consider what others think of them.

The same goes for certain companies and organizations. Just because one organization is more focused on profit-making than helping those less fortunate doesn't mean that all organizations operate that way. There is an attitude towards most organizations that they are all crooked in one way or another. Not so!

As another example, there's a widespread belief that postal workers are lazy. I remember seeing a cartoon of a customer walking into a post office. As he approached the counter, he noticed a sign that read "Closed." When the customer asked the clerk behind the counter about the closed sign, the response was, "Sorry, I don't know if we are on break, on strike or on vacation." But just go and visit a facility during the holidays and you will see how busy, productive and customer-friendly postal workers really are.

People would be better off keeping their eyes and ears open and their mouths closed—and for God's sake, take off the blinders. You may learn something if you do that will change your attitude in a positive manner.

# B

Bar Code Up
Batteries
Be Friendly to Your Neighbours
Black-and-White Pictures
Bucket List
Buy and Then Find

# Bar Code Up

Have you ever been in line waiting to pay for your purchase and for some unknown reason you are delayed because of a person at the cash register? Normally it's a price check, a return, not enough cash, a wrong entry by a cashier or a refused credit or debit card—but it now becomes a disagreement between two people, leading to delay and inconvenience for you.

Although you can't control how other people handle these situations, there's one thing you can do to make your purchase experience easier. Let's use a big-box store as an example—like Home Depot, Ikea or Walmart—where there are big-ticket items and at times many items in your cart. I try to put items in my cart with the bar code up so it is easy for the cashier to scan them. There's no fumbling around trying to find the code, and no need to move or remove the item from the cart to scan it. Some stores still have the scanning device attached to the computer by means of a sort of telephone cord that gets tangled up from time to time or dropped because it's stretched as far as it can. That leads to time lost, which can lead to loss of patience, which can lead to nasty thoughts and then nasty words and then arguments—and we don't want that to happen, now do we?

So do as I try to do and make the bar code easy for the cashier to read. These workers are underpaid and underappreciated as it is; making their job easier is a win-win for both parties. You get the satisfaction of knowing that a small gesture on your behalf made life a little easier for one person, and the cashier knows that not everyone takes his or her job for granted. Someone actually cares. We all deserve a little respect from our fellow human beings.

# Batteries

I can tell you from experience that it's not wise to leave any object with batteries in a car on very cold or extremely hot days. Camera, laptop and cellphone batteries will drain if left too long in the cold or even explode or burst in the heat. After batteries have been depleted in the cold, it seems to take longer to recharge them. They don't seem to keep a charge as long, especially camera batteries. It's a similar scenario with laptops.

It goes without saying that once a battery is fried from the heat, it will not be able to do anything but pay a trip to a garbage or recycling box. If the battery bursts in a camera, chances are the camera is also toast. Over the years, I have damaged two cameras, one laptop and one shaver. Learn from my mistakes. Those were very expensive lessons.

Do you know what happens when a case of pop is left in the trunk of a car for a couple of extremely hot days? First clue there is something wrong: buzzing sound. Second clue there is something wrong: popping sound that's similar to a gunshot. Third clue there is something wrong: a trunk full of soda, telling you it's too late.

# Be Friendly to Your Neighbours

Over the years and through many moves, I have been blessed with good neighbours—you know, the ones who mind their own business, take care of their property and are there to help you at a moment's notice when asked. A simple smile, a hello with a wave of the hand or a good-morning gesture can make all the difference in the world in how you get along with your neighbour.

When you are away on holidays, it's nice to have neighbours who will pick up the flyers from your driveway, retrieve your mail from the mailbox, water the grass or shovel snow. They may even park their car in your driveway to make your house look less abandoned and keep an eye on your place as a neighbourhood watch. I've had a neighbour in Brampton chase away people who were trying to dig up and steal flowers from our garden while we were at work.

One time in a heavy snowfall, while I was shovelling by hand, a neighbour across the road without any warning came with his new snow blower and proceeded to clear the sidewalk along the side of the house (corner lot). He didn't look for thanks or accolades; he just went back home and carried on his business. As neighbours, you do things without expecting rewards or favours in return.

Being friendly to our youth as neighbours has its benefits as well. You'll find that you get more respect from them if you show them respect as well. You give and you get—and once again, it's just being friendly. If you have an opportunity, take an interest in what they have to say. You may be surprised how much you can learn from a younger person.

The other benefit of being nice to the neighbours, which may not be noticed at the time, is the beginning of a bond of trust between you, and that is hard to come by. My bucket list trip is coming up as I write this, and it is so nice to know that my neighbours have already stepped up to help. For that, I am grateful and relieved that I can go away and not worry about a thing back home.

# Black-and-White Pictures

Most cameras today have high megapixels for quality, and touch-up features after a picture is taken to correct improper lighting, zooming, cropping, red eye and other imperfections. If that is not enough, the photo lab or even your own computer has programs that can do it all to make an everyday amateur photographer such as myself look like a world-renowned pro. It seems that Photoshop, as an example, can do wonders to a butchered picture and turn it into a ribbon-winning photo.

Recently, while looking for a waterproof camera to take with me on my upcoming bucket-list trip, it was pointed out to me that one of the features—which is now becoming more common with cameras these days—is the ability to take pictures in black and white or partially in black and white. The effect that a black-and-white picture can have is astounding when you think about it.

Have you ever seen an old black-and-white picture and stopped to look at it a little closer—not only to wonder at the main purpose of the picture but to take in the entire scene as if it was a jigsaw puzzle? Too many of these things of beauty have slipped away from me over the years, but the ones I have are very dear to me. When objects are shown without colour, one can't help but wonder about the picture's true meaning.

I can't speak for everyone, but when I look at one of these photos, there is a tendency to think a little more especially about the time in which the photo was taken. It amazes me how far advanced we are now. Just look at the cars, buildings, street signs, clothes and sporting events as examples, and you can't help but marvel at how far technology has come—although I truly believe that somehow we are also destroying this wonderful planet that we are using temporarily as our home.

To prove my point and have a little fun, try to get a hold of a few old-fashioned black-and-white photos. If you don't have any, there are books you can get a hold of. Take a colour picture of a similar scene and put them side by side. You will be amazed by both the differences and the similarities. Either way, it will have an impact on how you look at pictures and give you a different perspective on how to take them.

# Bucket List

In 2007, there was a movie out called *The Bucket List* starring Jack Nicholson and Morgan Freeman. The actors portrayed two different people with one thing in common: a desire to do specific things on a list before they passed away—"kicked the bucket"—due to a similar illness.

It took me a while to put my own bucket list together, and although I haven't crossed off many items yet, they are beginning to happen. My list is as follows:

1. Visit the Galapagos Islands. My boyhood hero was Charles Darwin.
2. Go to Africa, hunt with a camera and live outdoors while doing it.
3. Learn to play the harmonica.
4. Write a book for family and friends. If you are reading this, assume it's been done.
5. Travel to Alaska and see the icebergs before they disappear entirely.
6. Ride a motorcycle. Someone close to me says this will be over her dead body, so I may have to wait a while.
7. Make a hole in one playing golf. (I can just hear my friends Yasu, Kiran and Nam chuckling over this one.)
8. Volunteer in a poor country helping children.
9. Be elected to a seat on the city council. (Maybe 2018.)
10. Get over my fear of heights sufficiently to do the CN Tower Walk the Edge.
11. Fly a plane. I did attempt this in my early twenties, but on my very first solo flight I was told that one of my wheels just fell off and I would have to make a crash landing—all this at approximately 2,000 feet. I perfectly landed the plane, although I did a job on the grass. After I explained what had happened, filled out the report, answered a few questions

and asked a few questions, I very quietly got up from my chair, put down my cup of coffee (which I wore more than drank because of my shaking) and casually walked out of the hangar, never to return.

By the time you read this book, at least two of these adventures will be completed. My family and friends will know which ones. There will be more coming when I think of them, but it's a start. As children, we all have dreams, so why can't adults as well? These dreams give us hope and a reason to work hard so we are able to enjoy a few luxuries in life.

It's always fun to learn, enjoy new experiences and break out of the normal way of life (boring at times) to be adventurous. At least that's my point of view. I want to live and be part of the adventure, not see pictures or read about it in a book or watch a movie in which we all put ourselves in those roles. Just do it while you are physically able to say you've done it, not watched it or read about it. I have learned that putting things off until later doesn't work, as things happen beyond your control that can prevent you from achieving your bucket list. Just do it! In life, we all have to-do lists, so why not have one called a bucket list?

Life is too short. It's a privilege to enjoy, but it can be snatched away at a moment's notice. No one knows how long he or she is going to be around, so enjoy life now.

# Buy and Then Find

How many times have you misplaced or forgotten that you have a particular item somewhere close by and then proceeded to go out and buy another one (which takes time, effort and of course money)—only to find that once you return home, and probably after you've torn the packaging off and used it to a point where you can't return it, you find the misplaced or forgotten one. To make matters worse, you probably found this item while looking for another displaced item. Frustrating to say the least.

My suggestion is, do not look too hard for misplaced items. Just go out and buy another one. When you bring it home, place it in an obvious place where it can be seen by everyone. Just before you get into the packaging, take another look for the misplaced original. You will be surprised how fast you will find that piece. It will be a lot easier and less stressful to make the return to the store with original untouched packaging and a receipt compared to bringing back the item in packaging that looks like it came out of a meat grinder. They look at you funny at the counter if you try that.

# C

Camera Kept Handy
Car Keys
Car Lights
Change
Close Friend
Cloth Comes in Handy
Clothes Ready
Clothes—Try Something Different
Cost of Food

# Camera Kept Handy

With cellphones and tablets doing similar, if not the same, things as most cameras these days, it seems redundant to always have a camera with you for that special "Kodak moment," as the expression goes.

Still, I always have a camera in my car, since it's so easy to pull over safely onto the shoulder for a once-in-a-lifetime picture or just a shot of something different. To me, cellphones are phones, and as long as I can call someone or receive a call, I am a happy camper with no interest in whatever else the cellphone can do.

From my office in Bolton, I travel 40 kilometres on Highway 50 to and from my home in Alliston. Along the way, I pass farms, ponds and old building. There have been times I've seen a hawk gliding gently above, looking for prey, or staring down while perched on a pole; or horses gently prancing across a farmer's field; or cows grazing together in a herd near the road. That's just on my way to and from work.

The camera also comes with me when I play golf with friends or co-workers, and I use it to capture the lighter or silly side of the day. Pictures are priceless—and yours for the taking at the snap of a button.

# Car Keys

All humans, especially the male of the species, have at one time or another had a memory lapse—commonly known as a brain fart—and forgotten something of real importance. It could be as simple as forgetting to take the garbage out, forgetting a doctor's appointment or forgetting someone's birthday. (Although if it's your wife's birthday, it's not that simple anymore. You may as well forget to go home for a bit.)

There have been a few times, if memory serves me right, that my car keys disappeared without warning, and at the most inopportune time—such as when I was leaving a mall after the stores had closed and the majority of other shoppers had left (there goes my chance of getting help), just about to leave a sports venue as a coach (responsible for bringing home not only my own child but a couple of teammates) or exiting after a movie at a drive-in (older people know about those places) and I had to get my girlfriend home on time. It doesn't matter where you lost or misplaced your keys—it is almost always embarrassing and nearly always requires an explanation of how this could happen. Your ego gets knocked down a bit, and your reputation as a responsible person is scarred just a little.

That is why there is a set of keys hidden on the exterior of both my cars, although I will not say where just in case there is one unscrupulous person out there who knows where I live. Highly doubtful, but I'm not taking any chances. I have had to use those lifesavers on two occasions. Although I always eventually find my keys when my memory kicks in as to where they were placed, it's nice to know that a backup plan is available. The same is true for my house key, which is outside of my home in a very secure and inconspicuous location yet easy to find if needed. Again, no one knows where it is. I hope I don't forget.

# Car Lights

From time to time while sitting in my car—whether at home in my driveway or in the office parking lot—I will occasionally test all of my lights, making sure they work. I also check the signals by properly turning them on and off and watching for their reflection against the walls of my home or office building. If time permits (and it should, considering it takes only a couple of minutes to do the entire exercise), turn your car around and do the other set of lights and signals. This works better at night. As another old saying goes, "An ounce of prevention is worth a pound of cure."

Doing this exercise once in a while can save you from the nuisance of people flashing their lights at you because yours don't work or are starting to malfunction. Drivers and pedestrians may give you not only visual images but vulgar words to make you aware that your signal lights are not working, and you risk being horned to death with high beams coming at you from the rear because your tail lights are not functioning for whatever reason. You'll also avoid possible fines, which could have an impact on your insurance premiums.

# Change

How many times have you seen a person in a convenience store, for example, go to purchase an item that costs less than two dollars with a fifty- or even a hundred-dollar bill, and then stand there anxiously waiting for change? I remember one early morning at a Country Style Donut Shop on Highway 50 in Brampton. I was standing behind a teenage girl who asked for a bottle of water and handed a hundred-dollar bill to the clerk. I asked the young lady, "Why such a large bill?"

She replied, "That's what my parents gave me, and I need change for the bus."

I'm sure these small independent outlets don't carry that kind of change, especially first thing in the morning right after opening. People should have a little consideration for small businesses. Think of the little guy for a change (no pun intended).

Handing over a little extra when you pay can help to make the change you receive more manageable. Let's say your purchase comes to $5.07. You hand the clerk a twenty-dollar bill and wait for the change. Here it comes: $14.93 in all sizes possible. Let me see if I can get this right. You should receive as follows:

- 1 ten-dollar bill
- 2 toonies
- 3 quarters
- 1 dime
- 1 nickel
- 3 pennies (although by the time I finish this book, pennies will be phased out and no longer part of our currency)

On the other hand, if you added a dime when you handed over your twenty-dollar bill, your change would be as follows:

- 1 ten-dollar bill
- 1 five-dollar bill
- 3 pennies

I always try to carry a little change with me when I go somewhere, just in case it's needed. I have been told a number of times that it is greatly appreciated, and I wish others could be as thoughtful. It may sound like a small thing to you, but it means a lot to others.

# Close Friend

It's great to have a lot of friends, but too often, they can't be found in time of need. Whether the need is for financial assistance, moral support, emergency help, a visit while incapacitated or someone to talk to about a very personal matter, these so-called friends are nowhere to be seen. The word *friend* now means acquaintance or fair-weather friend.

When my son, who for reasons I don't need to go into here had to go away for a while (and I don't mean to jail), asked me, "What about my friends?" I told him that if they were true friends, they'd be here when he came back. Sadly, during the six months he was gone, not once did any of these so-called friends phone to ask how he was doing. They seemed to have fallen off the face of the earth.

I personally moved around a lot while growing up, and because of my workload and living situation (not at home), there was no time to connect with a true friend, although I had a lot of acquaintances in high school and on sports teams. When I started my first job after high school at a firm known as CPS on Strachan Avenue in Toronto, I got to know a man who was 10 years older than I was. His name was Yasuhiko Asai—Yasu for short. A little while later, another man, Kwan Kwok, was hired as a draftsman to help me. Who knew they would both become my lifelong friends?

We've known each other since 1970 and still are quite close today, or were until Kwan passed away from cancer in 2009. He may be gone physically, but he remains part of our trio. The following are just a few of our adventures, in no particular order:

- picking apples while golfing
- supper at Four Winds Drive
- bowling
- playing cards
- discussing news topics
- working together at two different companies at two different times

- Halloween parties
- Christmas together every year
- family birthdays
- outings
- driving lessons
- weddings
- family gatherings
- bar-hopping (even though Kwan did not drink)

Yasu and Kwan have been there for me through thick and thin, and even though I selfishly disappeared for a few years, I knew they would be there when I was ready, and I was right. I never took them for granted, and although I felt guilty for some time, they never held it against me. That's what friends do—I mean real, true friends. I will go a step further and call them my brothers.

Even to this day, Yasu and I reminisce about Kwan and the influence he had on our lives. His children, Michelle and Leo, are growing up just like their father: strong, smart, kind and trustworthy, with a great sense of humour. You can see the positive influence their dad had on his children. Kwan similarly influenced Yasu and myself to become stronger and better people on every level of daily life.

Yasu and I continue to grow closer over the years and still act silly at times. I guess the old adage suggesting that you should "always have a little bit of child inside you" is really true for us. I think we forget at times that we are adults and should act as such.

I will say very honestly and sincerely "Yasu, when the time comes, I hope I go first, because I don't think I could survive without your friendship." It may sound selfish, but it's very, very honest.

# Cloth Comes in Handy

When you're meeting a potential client, pursuing a job interview, going on a first date or attending a formal function, there is nothing more embarrassing to a man trying to make a good first impression than having it pointed out to him that his shoes are not up to standards of cleanliness for the occasion. Even if no one says anything, just a little stare can make him humble and embarrassed.

That first impression could make or break a deal, a job, a second date or another invitation, depending on how much of an impression you make. Why mess it up with your shoes? A cloth, shoe polish and wet wipes are always found in my car wherever I go, just in case.

The cloth comes in handy for ridding shoes of dust and scuff marks. All it takes to correct that little yet significant mark is a quick scan with your eyes immediately before entering any of the above-mentioned scenarios. If you can be wise enough to check before you leave your home, office or car, your shoes can be made perfect with a little shoe polish if need be.

I never really thought about this topic or realized its importance when I was younger until a doctor mentioned my new shoes and how good they looked. I was in his office getting my knee looked over at the time, and maybe a week after that I was told the same thing by a young woman. That's when it hit me that I should always be aware of my appearance in public.

On the other hand, there is an old saying that goes something like, "The bigger the shoe the larger the ..." Maybe she was just checking me out. I have never been that lucky, and I do not parade around looking for it.

# Clothes Ready

This one came to light a few summers ago when there was a power outage in Toronto and surrounding areas. I believe it began at around four o'clock on a Thursday afternoon, August 14, 2003, and lasted for a couple of days. I had planned on doing something before that in case of an emergency, but there is a tendency to procrastinate and this time was no different.

Since that outage, I have made sure that my clothes are properly set out before I go to bed so they are at least handy in the morning. I don't want to look like an idiot with oddball colours or different socks or, worse, stumble around the bedroom banging into walls and knocking over lamps in my effort to find things in the dark. There have been times when I went to the office with a few scratches, cuts and bruises from my walks around the house. Please don't even think about shaving.

The power outage of Christmas 2013, of which we were spared the hardships, reemphasized my need to be prepared no matter what the case may be. Mother Nature is finally fed up with what we are doing to her planet and gives us these reminders and challenges so we can wake up and do something about it. One day, it may be a permanent test. Not in my time, but maybe someday. Something to think about, seriously.

# Clothes—Try Something Different

Quite a few years ago, being told that my attire was boring kind of struck a blow to my ego, but at the same time it opened my eyes to a whole new experience of fashion. Although I was quite comfortable with my coordinated outfits with matching colours for shirts and pants—simple, casual outfits that blended in with those around me—it was time to try the advice of those close to me and be a little adventurous.

Stepping out of your comfort zone takes a bit of getting used to, and there were and still are times when I say to myself, *What were you thinking?* or *Why are people wearing sunglasses when they look at me?* Talk about standing out like a sore thumb. I trusted the people making these suggestions, but it seemed the clothes were getting brighter and brighter as time went on. There were days when I felt like a golfer on the PGA course whose clothes were set out for him by a colour-blind coordinator of fashion. *Outlandish, outrageous, WTF* were some of the words that came to mind.

That is, until I visited the Philippines. It was there that my attitude changed. It seemed the more colourful you were, the more attractive you were, and that's not because I'm white.

Let me tell you, the people in the Philippines, in my personal opinion, are the most beautiful in the world. They know how to draw attention to themselves with their outfits. Children, teenagers, young adults, parents, retail and office workers—they know fashion and are not afraid to show it.

The newer the fashion, the faster it gets out to the street. Ever since my first trip to the Philippines, the bar for total boredom has dropped. There are times when being neutral is still the way to be on a daily basis, but every once in a while try to spice it up with a little colour to set yourself apart from the person beside you. When you go out at night, show your fun and adventurous side. The looks you'll get and the comments you'll hear may surprise you.

Comments on my wardrobe have been mostly positive so far. When I get a negative look, I just think, *Get over it and quit being a stick-in-the-mud* or *They're just jealous that they can't let their guard down and be themselves.*

In short, when you try something to make yourself feel good, to heck with those who think otherwise. As the saying goes, "When you feel good, those around you feel good, and that makes everything you do worth it."

# Cost of Food

The cost of food or the constantly rising price of gas may seem like a reason to get a little angry, upset and stressed—but when you think about it, at least we can afford to buy food for the family and drive around in a car that enables us to get from point A to point B in a convenient and timely manner.

A lot of people (single and/or married with children) do not have that luxury or privilege. I'm sure you've noticed, as I have, people waiting at a bus or streetcar stop very early in the morning in bitter cold weather, trying to get to their minimum-wage jobs and work their rear ends off to barely make enough after taxes to put food on the table, a roof over their heads and basic clothing on their children. Once their workday is done, they must reverse the morning cycle and wait at the bus stop again to get home. They can ill afford to miss a day of work; missing work may mean a missed meal for the family.

We can sit back and enjoy our coffee and scan the flyers in our weekly papers to find out where the deals are, but the less fortunate do not have the luxury of shopping around. They must take what they can find and hope that there is enough food to go around. It actually makes me shake my head in disgust when I hear people complain about the cost of food or the cost of gas or the cost of running their car or the cost of their designer clothes or the cost of their trip.

Maybe if we sacrifice all or some of these privileges for a time, we can appreciate how fortunate we are to have the luxuries we take for granted. But I doubt people would be willing to do that. It's too much of a sacrifice.

As a young person, I was the one with no home and no one to guide me, as I took care of myself from age 13 (no silver spoon here). Although I enjoy certain privileges today, they are not and never will be taken for granted, as I know they can be taken away in a heartbeat.

What I will say is that if sh*t happens and we have to start over as a society, I can guarantee you that the name *Gordon* is synonymous with the word *survivor*. There is no need for me to worry. Can you say the same?

# D

Do Not Delete Pictures
Do Not Feel Sorry for Yourself
Do Not Get Upset in Traffic
Do Not Judge People
Do Not Jump to Conclusions
Do Not Pick Sides
Do Not Procrastinate
Do Not Wish Time Would Hurry
Do Things Properly
Doctors and Dentists
Donate Your Time

# Do Not Delete Pictures

From personal experience, I advise you: do not delete your pictures from your camera until you have saved them somewhere else, such as another device, a CD or as actual prints. I used to have a tendency to delete pictures once they were in the processing stage—being reproduced at a photo lab, for example, which can be done in as little as an hour.

Computer technology is great, but there is still a human component involved somewhere in the process. Where humans are involved, there is a chance of human error. I have seen a few mishaps over the years, and I am sure there are others ahead for me to experience. For example, the store may inadvertently give your pictures to someone else because someone behind the counter grabbed the wrong package or misread the claim number. If the other person is honest, your photos will be returned, and this will be a minor inconvenience. If not, your photos are gone.

Photos can also get lost in the photo lab's computer. They can be deleted accidentally, or you may get the wrong quality or size of prints. You may have to start over. Let's not forget that, when talking about human error, we must look at ourselves as well. I have left the store, put the envelope of these prized possessions on top of my car in order to search for my keys and then driven away without realizing that the package of prints never made it inside the car. Embarrassing, but it happens.

So my word to you would be keep the pictures on your memory card, and buy another one if need be. You just never know.

# Do Not Feel Sorry for Yourself

Growing up on my own (before I turned 14), there were times when thoughts of *why me, what's the use, alone again, it's not fair* or *what's next* were a common way of thinking on a daily basis. Reality set in one day after a scary thought came into my head: *I don't want to be here anymore.* Although I considered suicide, it finally dawned on me that life is what you make of it. If you do nothing, you receive nothing.

Life is too short to feel sorry for yourself. If you want something, go for it. Don't wait for it to come to you. Not everything is going to be handed to you on a silver platter, and not everyone is born with a silver spoon in his mouth, so to speak. Some people have to work at it. They are known as survivors. I am a survivor.

Remember that no matter how horrible a situation is—whether it be a financial crisis, a relationship failure or something as simple as being late for a job interview or a date due to traffic—there is always someone else worse off than you. I'll share with you the exact scenario that brought me to my senses about self-pity and life in general.

I was going to attend a sporting event, and I was agitated because time was becoming a factor. I was distraught that I might miss the event altogether because of somebody's stupidity on the road. Just as I drew close to the source of the traffic jam, it became evident that this was no normal accident. When I saw a white sheet being placed completely over a lifeless body, I realized that there's always tomorrow to do something special, visit somebody or have fun. For that person under the sheet, it was all over. Suddenly, the selfishness and self-pity that seemed to be smothering me became unjustifiable.

Later that evening, while watching the local news, I learned that the person under the sheet was a 5-year-old boy. The tears flowed for quite some time that night just thinking of the little boy, and that's when it really sank in. Life is a privilege that can be snatched away in a heartbeat with no warning, so it's best to enjoy it rather than complain about it.

# Do Not Get Upset in Traffic

We are all human when it comes to living and experiencing life. We all make mistakes and bad decisions. We have little accidents from time to time, and we can sit back and admit to these brain-fart moments, so to speak. But when we get behind a steering wheel, that human being who understands mistakes and is eager to forgive and forget is replaced by a Neanderthal.

Our normal happy face with a warm smile and a friendly nod—as if saying "nice to see you" and "have a great day"—mutates into an abnormal grimacing face full of anger—as if saying "get the hell out of my way" and flipping a middle finger. Why are we like that?

If you have a problem with slow drivers, why get mad and sound the horn—or, even worse, zigzag in and out of traffic just to beat someone to the next red light? Why not just leave a few moments earlier and eliminate the need to act silly and careless? Is that too simple a solution? It would be a much better and safer road to drive on if we thought a little more before we sat behind the wheel.

# Do Not Judge People

Why is it that we are so quick to judge people by their appearance or because of our biases and prejudices? The saying, if I'm not mistaken, goes something like, "Do not judge a book by its cover."

Growing up, it was difficult for me to land a part-time job because my long hair (hippie days) was unacceptable in the workplace back in the sixties. I was fortunate to finally get a job working for the TTC (Hillcrest) at the Bay and Dundas bus terminal through my high school guidance department. Even then, there was one condition, and that was to lose any hair below the neckline. It was nice to know that someone had not only spoken up for me but also seen through my appearance and given me the opportunity to prove myself. I made the most of it.

That's where I quickly learned to accept people for who they are, regardless of their appearance, colour and religion. To me, it's what is inside a person's head, not what you see on the outside. Get to know people by talking to them; be attentive to their expressions and knowledge. It may surprise you how intelligent they are, how compassionate they are, how eager they are to learn and how willing they are to help.

I reinforced that with my children as they were growing up, and it shows today. Everyone should be treated with the respect and dignity that we all deserve. It's no fun being rejected all the time just because of your hair colour and length, or your style of clothing. These are just expressions of ourselves. Remember that inside, these people you judge are most likely the same as you: hardworking, caring, compassionate, committed and family-loving. When they make a statement, it is peacefully and methodically thought out. That's something to think about.

# Do Not Jump to Conclusions

Any way you want to look at it, most of us have been guilty of jumping to conclusions at one time or another. We need to remember the saying goes something like, "Listen with intelligence in mind rather than speaking with nothing in mind."

A prime example would be the thoughts that used to automatically come to mind whenever I saw bikers all decked out in their leathers noisily flying along the highway to hang out at bars or patios like those at the Dardanella Restaurant in Wasaga Beach. At first, I would feel intimidated and fearful. But that first impression of tough-looking guys you would not want to mingle with could not be further from the truth. They are the most gentle, carefree, conservative, caring group of men out there. Their bike rides are often for a good cause, like fundraising for charities that help hospitals, children's camps, and the homeless. I can guarantee you that if asked to help, they would not hesitate. All they would ask in reply would be where and when.

Another example: I used to feel critical of the media or anyone who tried to give a one-sided story, believing that these people just dig to find dirt on someone, stopping at nothing to create a story they can sell, whether it's true or not, with no regard for the innocent people involved. I was a supporter of a prominent and well-respected local politician and would defend him when allegations first came out against him. But after so many discoveries, the truth was exposed about his abuse and other problems. I went from anger at the media to applauding those people for giving me the truth. From then on, I have resolved to listen first and not pass judgment until I know all the facts.

# Do Not Pick Sides

I have had many experiences of trying to offer advice or intervene in family squabbles. Inevitably, I end up adding more fuel to the fire rather than extinguishing the flames. I will pass on a wee bit of advice to those who have thought of being an adjudicator in such situations: No matter what you do, it will come back to bite you in the butt one way or another. You will either have both parties turn on you, or one turn against you and the other tell you to mind your own business. You can't win.

One example that comes to mind involved a discussion about teachers and their protest or walkout or whatever. Names will be left out for fear of reprimand or potential legal repercussions. In my family, anything is possible.

I believe it was Thanksgiving or Christmas, and all was going well. There were, I believe, five teachers among us. They were discussing recent events in separate school boards, and accusations were flying, with everyone talking and nobody listening—typical in this family. The general theme was that everyone was to blame except the teachers themselves.

For some reason, I threw my two cents in, saying that not everyone was blaming or hating the teachers. I mentioned that I had been supporting teachers by bringing coffee and biscuits to them as they walked around the school during their strike or demonstration. After all, I was an elected official of the PTA of another school, the one my daughter attended—the first male elected, I will proudly add.

Anyway, a teacher who thought I was against her lambasted me. She wouldn't stop yapping at me and wouldn't listen to reason. When her sister, a non-teacher, tried to clear up the matter, she was also snapped at. I gave up and quietly walked away while the others jostled for position. Nobody was backing down.

There's a silver lining here, though, if you think a bit. If someone is mad at you, chances are that person won't be seeking you out any time soon to talk to you. That, my friend, is heaven.

# Do Not Procrastinate

For many, many, many years, procrastination was an integral part of my lifestyle. On many occasions, that was an unfortunate fact. I would miss family functions only to find out later that somebody had passed away shortly after, and I would never have a chance to see that person again.

My last living aunt (Betty) was anxious to see my firstborn, Jason. who was born in March 1977. I kept promising that she would be able to hold him in her arms before he got too big, but it never happened. There was always something more important on my agenda—or maybe, just maybe, I couldn't be bothered to sacrifice my time just to put a smile on my aunt's face. Shame on me!

The same could be said about a good friend of mine who passed away a few years ago of cancer. Kwan had always been there for me and my family. There was never a moment in his life when he couldn't make time for us. Every birthday, Christmas, funeral, dinner—he always could be counted on to enjoy and share laughter or tears. Unfortunately, there were years when I disappeared from his life. My own selfishness led me astray, and I wasn't man enough to correct the situation. Over time, maturity and common sense prevailed, but I could not get back the time I could have been spending with such a wonderful human. I carry a burden of guilt, thinking of my Aunt Betty and Kwan from time to time. It's a hard guilt to get rid of. It seems to linger on.

Don't put off doing something for someone regardless of how miniscule it may seem to you. Whether it is a helping hand or a visit to a friend or a family member, please follow through today, not tomorrow. As we all know, tomorrow may never come. Personally speaking, the guilt can be heavy, and it stays with you.

# Do Not Wish Time Would Hurry

How many times have you said to yourself, *I wish I could make time go faster* or *I can't wait another minute*? Whether young or old, we have all said something to that effect more times than we would like to admit. See if any of the following sound familiar:

- A child wants Christmas to be here tomorrow, and it's only the beginning of November.
- A teenager wants Friday to be here sooner than it is, as he or she is looking for a great night out with friends.
- Parents can't wait for bedtime so they can enjoy what little time is left in the evening without all the noise and commotion children can cause.
- Seniors want it to be five in the evening so they can have dinner or eleven at night so they can go to bed.

For the longest time, these scenarios were part of my life. There was a time when a lack of patience ruled the roost, so to speak. Over the years, I have mellowed (or so I like to think), and for the most part I've become more laid-back; the few exceptions have become a reminder that life is short and should be enjoyed on a daily basis, not worrying about what will happen in the near future.

Every moment of every day should be cherished and treasured with the same exuberance and excitement as if you had just won the lottery, moved into to your first home, celebrated the birth of your first child or purchased a new car. So what if it rains on your outing? Make the best and enjoy whatever life brings. Remember, life is a privilege that can be taken away at a moment's notice, without warning. We are all here for a short time, so make every moment count. Personally, I am extremely happy to just wake up every day so as I can enjoy the simple things in life. If they happen to involve family or good friends, that's a bonus.

# Do Things Properly

You have no idea how many times I've rushed through something just to get it out of the way or to impress someone, without reading instructions or following all the necessary steps, and with no consideration for the consequences of not doing it properly. Maybe it's a guy thing. We tend to ignore proper procedure because in our minds, we know better. That is the wrong attitude to take.

Instructions are there for a reason, and it's best to abide by them. It will be better for you in the long run. Even the pros follow instructions. They can't afford careless mistakes because they are responsible and liable for them. Going back for a repair takes time, and as we all know, time is money. My advice would be to listen to the pros.

I took a shortcut once when putting a concrete patio in my backyard. Unfortunately, I did not listen to the few words of advice I was given. I thought to myself, *I know how to save a few bucks and some time so let's skip a couple of steps*. Those couple of steps saved me a little change at the time, but I paid dearly for it the following year. To make a long story short, using less gravel and no plastic layer under the concrete caused cracking and weeds. Those in the business will know what that means.

But let me tell you a funny story. My father, a Scotsman, liked to indulge in spirits (mainly beer), and when you put that together with a nagging wife (his second), it is a recipe for disaster. After quite a few beers and a few words of displeasure, my dad decided to do a job he should have done sober, and that was laying floor tiles at the cottage. Back then, before peel-and-stick, you had to use glue when putting in tiles. He completed the room in record time, only to discover the next morning that the tile patterns did not match, and some of the tiles were upside down. Not only did he have to pull up the tiles—destroying some in the process—and clean and redo what he did the day before, but all of this had to be done while he was suffering a severe hangover. I disappeared to the beach for the day.

This is not to be confused with "Instructions Should Be Read" because some projects do not come with any instructions, just through experience or learning from others and common sense.

# Doctors and Dentists

Doctors and dentists seem to be stereotyped, or maybe stigmatized, as aloof and superior beings. Why are we so intimidated by someone in a white doctor's cloak or a lab coat? They are there to help us, whether to prescribe medicine for a cold or antibiotics for an infection, to put a few stitches in a deep cut, to repair a broken bone, to mend an ailing heart, to remove tumours or to help us understand life.

The following are some of the reasons I've had to visit these professionals for repair or advice:

- scratched retina
- laser surgery on eye
- pulling a nail from my hand
- knee issues galore
- cartilage repair
- cartilage repair, again
- meniscus tear and repair
- depression
- replacement of teeth
- emergency visits to release fluid buildup in knees
- stitches in tongue
- cracked ribs
- minor heart worries (twice)
- head issues (not including eye)
- broken thumb

Most of these visits took place before I was 25, so as you can see, I have had more than my share of experiences with professionals. Believe it or not, there has been a comfort and trust between most of them and myself—with the exception of one. I guess that relates to my experience as a child, of which I will say no more.

Someone once told me that sh*t happens, so get over it. Unless you have been victimized in your life by someone in authority, you have no idea how hard it is to move forward. It's traumatizing—demoralizing to say the least. Feelings of depression and anxiety set in 24-7, and trust is thrown out the window.

I have been extremely fortunate and blessed to have been with my dentist, Dr. Wuls, for almost forty years now. It may sound silly, but I still need to be in unbearable pain before I'll pick up the phone to make an appointment. Dr. Wuls and his assistant, Sharon, along with Adrienne have been helpful in every way possible when it comes to my mouth. They are very pleasant, understanding and respectful of my needs; they have always acted in a very professional manner when it comes to making me feel relaxed and at ease from the moment I walk through the front door with a problem to the moment I leave through that same door totally ready to tackle the world.

They are focused from the get-go and are not satisfied with just getting by. They strive to do their best every time and always push for supreme results. Other patients will agree with me, I'm sure. A few years ago, I noticed a sign in his office that reads "Genius at Work." One might think that he has a swelled head, but on the contrary, I find him to be a true gentleman, with true care and concern for his patients. That sets him apart from the ones who are there more for the money and the ego than their patients' well-being.

Even though I am sure that Dr. Wuls does better than okay financially (and deservedly so), he does not show that side. He comes across as a confident yet humble professional with a sense of humour—and that is very much appreciated. I am confident that there are more out there like Dr. Wuls, and I am lucky to have him as my dentist. With him there is no fear, just procrastination on my part.

I wish that other doctors and dentists would get off their high horse or pedestal and listen to what is being said to them with attentive ears instead of getting their ego bruised when someone points out that they may be wrong or there is an alternative solution. We are all human, after all, and should treat one another with respect. Let's not forget that it's our bodies they are playing God with. Doctors don't know everything.

I tell my children not to waste time going to emergency with petty things like a runny nose, a small headache or a tiny cut. The doctors' time is much too valuable to spend on non-emergency problems. If and when you do have to go, however, don't be afraid to ask questions, and don't be embarrassed. Be honest about the past, as to how and why you got there. Doctors for the most part do not pass judgment. Their main focus is on figuring out what ails you and fixing it, plain and simple.

I have the utmost respect for these professionals, but they are not God, although some clearly think they are. And don't get me started with lawyers. After all, there may be children reading this book. I can guarantee you that swear words would be flying, and I can't leave that as a memory for my grandchildren.

# Donate Your Time

Growing up on the streets of Toronto during my early to mid-teen years (14 to 17) gave me not only an idea of how harsh life could be but also an appreciation of what I have today and an admiration of those who are out there now just trying to survive. I have learned not to judge others by their looks but will instead try to understand and imagine what has brought them to their current reality. There are two sides to every story, and not every side is a fairy-tale upbringing tossed aside due to whatever we want to believe happened. We have a tendency to suspect all homeless people are involved with drugs, gambling and booze—that they want or need their addiction, whatever the type.

I believe everyone should donate to places like Covenant House, the Good Shepard, Salvation Army, local hostels, Sick Kids and animal shelters. To me, donating means more than just writing a cheque—we should also give time to these worthy causes. That might mean helping in the soup kitchen of a local hostel, giving rides to seniors for doctors' appointments, spending time with those who struggle and sharing stories to learn about someone's past. Some people crave the opportunity to tell their stories. It is very rewarding to me to listen intently, hear and understand.

There should not be one day that goes by that we don't learn something. We all should put our pride on a shelf for a bit to understand these people—not belittle, ignore or criticize them. They are human beings after all, just like you and me.

I pride myself on helping when I can, especially around the holidays. I have found it very rewarding and gratifying, to say the least—and you know what? It's free. It costs you nothing to put a smile on someone's face as well as your own face, knowing you have made someone's day better, no matter how miniscule your effort seems.

You don't have to announce it to the world that you do this, but if it can make others close to you think about doing something to help, then yes, let them know how it feels and the difference you are making. There is no need to brag about it. I truly believe that we all need reminders of how lucky and fortunate we are to have what we have. It seems that we all brag about what we have and complain about the luxuries we're missing. As a society, we seem to take life for granted—and feel that it owes us. Nothing could be further from the truth.

Eyes Open

# Eyes Open

"Eyes open" should be expanded to read, "Eyes open, ears open, mouth shut." If you play your cards right and follow these instructions, you'll be surprised how much you can learn. I mean, every day is a wonderful experience to begin with, but there is always an opportunity and a vast array of knowledge just waiting to be shared and discovered—all of it free.

I have seen too many people who think they know it all. I am not going to mention names, because there are too many who are close to my family, and I really do not want to get myself into any more trouble. Plus, to be honest, I do not like to badmouth people behind their back in a book, or online, or to another person—it really isn't fair to the person I'm talking about. I do have my faults, but I can go to bed knowing I haven't hurt anyone physically, mentally, emotionally or financially.

I seem to have gotten off the track—what I am trying to say is, when you're in a group of people, try to listen and learn something. Maybe it will be a news topic, an investment tip, the score of a sports game the night before, information on an upcoming event or a sale item at a store, what someone's children have done, a review of a new product, a political viewpoint which could change your own—the list goes on and on.

I always suspect that a person who yaps all the time and tries to take control of a conversation has some sort of inferiority complex and is a little insecure. Take a look at all the great influential people of the world who are successful in life. They got there by being noticed and not looking for any acknowledgment or ego boost. They are leaders.

When you listen instead of talking, you create a little mystery about yourself. The less you say, the more confident you seem. That may bother some, but it intrigues me to want to learn more. The following are a few of my favourites along these lines:

- Warren Buffet
- Bill Gates
- Michael Jordan
- Jimmy Carter
- Nelson Mandela

I'm not saying we have to listen to powerful people—those with fancy cars, clothes and houses. In fact, most of those people are obnoxious and braggers, the type I tend not to socialize with and try to stay away from. Be aware that everyone has something to say, whether it be a co-worker, a family member, a server in a restaurant or even a child. We can learn a lot more than you think by listening to children—not enough credit is given to them, and they are smarter than you think.

Even listening to animals, you will learn something. When you hear constant chirping, whether it be a single bird or, more significantly, a group, you can bet the farm that the weather is about to change. Listen, observe and learn. Heck, even my dog Chelsea teaches me things. When I observe her actions and tail-wagging, I'm reminded that being happy and content is as simple as being around those you love. It may be a simple philosophy, but it works, and it really does not take much effort.

# F

Fish in a Jar
Flowers for No Reason
Friendship With Youth
Funerals

# Fish in a Jar

This may come across to some as weird, strange and eccentric—and you may choose to toss it aside without much thought—but I find that watching fish can be very relaxing. It's like going to therapy or yoga, if you think about it, and it's free. I find it to be soothing to the mind and cleansing to the soul.

When I am visiting my friends Yasu and Naomi at their home in Thornhill, I always sit on their couch for a few minutes and watch their aquarium filled with goldfish swimming free without a care or concern in the world. The fish seem very much at peace with themselves and their surroundings. Not that they have much choice, mind you. Their life and well-being can be summed up in four words: swim, eat, poop, sleep. What's wrong with that?

We as human beings should be content with what we have instead of trying to outdo each other and working ourselves crazy just to keep with up with the neighbours, or competing with each other to prove how much better we are. Why not be like our little buddies inside the aquarium—at peace with each other and getting along without worrying about anything? Enjoy the moment, as I always say.

# Flowers for No Reason

Giving flowers is almost a lost art these days. Remember how in all those old Western movies, a cowboy would come courting a young lady, bring her flowers, and ride off with her into the sunset to live happily ever after? Maybe I'm showing my age.

That seems to be a thing of the past. We as men take a lot for granted these days and are very conveniently forgetful of what is most important to us. Let's be honest: as men, we like to have our ego boosted or stroked every once in a while—and the same goes for women (although they don't seek it out like we do, and they don't get bruised when they don't get it). It is nice to feel thought of and appreciated by your partner from time to time. There doesn't have to be a reason, and it doesn't have to cost much—unless you consider a few minutes out of your hectic day costly.

I like to bring home fresh flowers from time to time. No reason, no guilt, no motive. It's just my small way of saying thank you for all that is done for me. We're talking about a very, very small gesture here on your behalf, just to make your significant other feel a little more important, wanted, respected and loved. We all crave that once in a while, whether we want to admit it or not.

I have been very fortunate to have a fantastic florist relatively close to my old office. If you are ever in the Woodbridge area (just north of Toronto) and are seeking any kind of arrangement, you have to visit Verona Florist on Whitmore Road. Joe, wife Dora and family have a very well-established business. It does not matter what you are looking for or for what occasion, you will find it there. They are very attentive of your needs and always give a great product with a very reasonable price. They are very efficient in having your purchase ready when you would like it. I've been going there for flowers for years.

I've visited Joe's for the poinsettias I give to the ladies in my office at Christmas as a small gesture of appreciation for the hard work they do all year; flowers for my daughter when she graduated from university; and arrangements for funerals, birthdays and anniversaries. All I have to do is phone, walk in, state the occasion and that's it. Not once have I been disappointed or felt like I paid too much.

I have mentioned to Joe a few times that if his store had been around when I was younger, I would have been lucky with the ladies more often. He is that good—if you don't believe me, just go there on Valentine's Day and see the crowd of men seeking flowers to bring home. Even if they don't get there on a regular basis, they do know where to go when needed. Thanks, Joe.

To sum this up, it does not cost much or take much effort to put a smile on your significant other's face. There are numerous ways you can show your love or concern, but this is my way, and as long as it's enjoyable to her, I will continue to do it. Not because I have to, but because I want to. She deserves to be put up on a pedestal every day.

# Friendship With Youth

Why is it that the older we get, the smarter we become? So they say, anyway. If that's really true, why are we the first ones to blame, criticize, belittle, ignore and abuse our youth?

If we old folks are so smart, shouldn't we be helping young people in their process of growing up to be just like us, or even better than us? That's coming from a parent's perspective. In all honesty, these children as we know them are our future. It is up to us as a society to nurture them, teach them, support them and offer them advice as best we can. We know they will make mistakes along the way; we all did growing up. As long as they learn or give the best effort they possibly can, that's all parents should ask of a child. That's part of growing up—the trials and tribulations of being young.

I tell this to my children all the time—especially Jason, who has two of his own, and Nicholas, who has three. Kids make noise, make messes, break things, write on things, say rude words, have temper tantrums, disobey their parents, interrupt at times, embarrass their parents, refuse to do homework, fail a subject, dent or scratch a car, tell a few lies, miss curfew, take a drink to fit in, try grass to fit in and so much more.

If parents tell me that they have a perfect child, without hesitation I will tell them that they are in denial and should man up to reality. Face the facts and admit that no one is perfect. I have always said that if a child sits and does everything he or she is told to do, then the worrying should start. Children and teenagers learn through their mistakes (we hope) and become better people for it. As parents, we should give kids a little slack. After all, we were all kids at one time or another, and you would be surprised at how much adults can learn by listening to and observing our youth.

Can you imagine if we, as mature parents, could keep our mouths closed once in a while and keep our ears and eyes open a little more? We might find that our kids make us more proud than we give them credit for. They are not stupid. They are focused, smart, innovative, passionate, committed, caring, constructive and determined. We should be proud of them and let them know how proud we are. Give them time and a little space, and they will find their niche in life and contribute to society in a positive and meaningful manner. I have faith and total belief in that.

A long time ago, I was inspired with a priest, Father John, who ran an addiction program in North York named Caritas. I hope I remember the words he used one time. If not, at least the meaning is still the same: "If your child does not study or put his or her own best effort into a test but still gets an A, he or she can do better. If your child studies and puts his or her best effort in a test and gets a C, then God bless them."

Before I forget, I will mention that I have four children in total: Jason, 38; Nicholas, 35; Andrew, 30; and Jennifer, 24, a recent graduate from OCAD.

# Funerals

Funerals can be intimidating, or in some cases downright frightening to people who cannot fathom the idea of standing in front of or looking at a dead body in a casket. Most people have good intentions of paying their respects, whether for a family member, a co-worker, a friend or a neighbour. But for some reason, they just don't want to be there, and it can be quite a challenge for them. To me, it's a wakeup call to once again say, "Stop and smell the roses." Your time will come, and you'll be the one pushing up daisies.

Funerals can be a way to celebrate life and remember the good times and the not-so-good times in addition to paying tribute to the deceased. There are opportunities to rekindle relationships with family and friends as well as starting up new ones with friends or strangers from the past. It is a time to celebrate, not to be sad.

I don't think it's a unique idea, but when my time comes to meet my maker, I already have the funeral planned out to save my family a little grief and work. How about preparing an ongoing video about your life and throwing in thoughts about how you perceive yourself? Do your own eulogy and have it played at the viewing for your funeral, or at a party. Remember to celebrate. All you need is a chair to sit on, a video camera on a tri-pod with a remote to start and stop the camera. After all, no one knows you better than yourself. Can you imagine what you could say and get away with after all those years of keeping inside you what you wanted to say about certain people? What can they do except turn red with embarrassment or red with anger? Let the world know that you got the last laugh and the last word. As the saying goes "Take it to the grave" now has a whole new meaning.

Guys who have been married a long time know what I'm talking about. Just in case my family is curious, to them I say it's already a work in progress and will be no-holds-barred, with no words or secrets taken to my grave. My life will be an open book, so be warned and be prepared to answer to others close to you.

# G

Gas Nozzle
Gas Up Before Bad Weather
Go for the Underdog

# Gas Nozzle

Since moving to Alliston in May of 2013 and commuting to my office in Toronto and (after a relocation in the spring of 2014) Bolton, I've been visiting the gas station much more often. It's a small price to pay for living in a fresh-air country-style small town, with a friendlier atmosphere and way of life than Toronto and the suburbs. On more than one occasion, though, in my haste to gas up and move on in a hurry, I've been a little careless, and long into my travels noticed a lingering odour of gas.

The first time this happened, I thought there may have been a puncture in my gas tank, but that lingering annoying stench was in the car with me. Then it dawned on me: I must have spilt a few drops somewhere on my clothes or my shoes or directly on my hands. Guess what—it was all three. You can wash your hands over and over until the sun goes down, but that smell stays for the longest time. For that reason, it's worth taking a few extra moments to lift the nozzle slowly out of the pump and immediately put it carefully and gently into the open part of the gas tank. Slowly squeeze the handle to start dispensing the fuel, and then and only then grab tight so as to fill up with a little speed.

Please pay attention, too, when the tank is almost full. A warning comes, as it seems someone is inside your tank and telling you "I am slowing down now, so please ease up on the handle so you don't overflow the tank and get gas inside the door, dripping down the side of your car and splashing a few drops on you, or all three." Tilt the nozzle a little, release the grip and once again slowly pull the nozzle out of the car and gently put it back, holding it away from your body, into the proper location on the pump. Sounds easy enough, doesn't it? It saves at lot of aggravation—not to mention cleaning bills—from not having the smell of gas on you. This makes for a better ride and a better day.

There is one more thing to do before you leave the gas station, and that is, "Get your receipt!" At a local gas station I frequented regularly a long time ago, not once but twice I was accused of not paying for the gas. Other patrons were nice enough to catch up to me a couple of blocks later and tell me the police had been called. Twice I went back to show the attendant my receipt, once with the police there. It was very embarrassing for him. The officer and I just shrugged our shoulders. Unreal!

# Gas Up Before Bad Weather

It happens to all of us at some time or another. You leave your house in the morning to go to work or leave your work at night to go home without thinking to check that gas gauge staring at you on the dash. Just when it's least convenient, you realize your mistake: *OMG, I should have put gas in the car.*

I drive on highways every day where there are not a lot of gas stations along the way. I know I have to check the gas level whenever I get behind the wheel. It only takes a moment to check and save myself many anxious moments along the way—or unnecessary, embarrassing times on the side of the road, especially in the winter when one never knows what Mother Nature may throw our way at a moment's notice. Bad weather brings bad road conditions which, combined with bad drivers, tend to cause accidents that in turn cause long delays. Even if you're just sitting in traffic, your car is using gas, and eventually the needle will start to move towards the letter *E*.

If you're not prepared, the delay can cause a lot of stress, as worrying about the mess and trying to resolve it and what it will cost can really do a number on you. And that's if you are by yourself. What if your family is with you for a planned trip that may now be ruined because of a silly and selfish oversight on your behalf? It can be devastating to say the least, so try to be a little more responsible and routinely check that gas gauge. It's a small thing to do.

Living outside of the city in a rural setting, I have learned very quickly to adapt to my surroundings. A lot of places close down early here, and that includes gas stations. That's why I always check on my way home the night before and fill up if necessary to ensure that I am ready to go with a full tank in the morning regardless of road conditions. There are times when I am on the road extremely early so as to get a jump on my daily deadlines, so by the time the gas stations are opening, I have already had my first cup of coffee while sitting at my desk, working on my drawings.

Location, location, location doesn't just apply to real estate. Knowing the location of nearby gas stations at all times—whether at work, at a restaurant, at a meeting—may seem to be a minuscule or insignificant detail, but it could possibly save you time and aggravation later. I will add that a quick check of washer fluid, tire pressure and wipers can be conceived of as preventive medicine. In fact, why not join CAA, as I have done, for the ultimate driving security, especially on used vehicles?

# Go for the Underdog

As someone who has lived in or near Toronto all of his life, this one comes easy to me. Anyone who knows about the history of sports in Hogtown can attest to the fact that we as sport fans are accustomed to losing franchises.

From the hapless Toronto Maple Leafs to the double-blue Toronto Argonauts to the Toronto Blue Jays, Raptor and FC, I don't think you can count all the major championships achieved by all of these teams combined on one hand over the last 20 years. Heck, the Leafs haven't won since 1967. I worked at the Gardens the last time they won the cup. Even the Raptors can't get past the second round (2000-2001). The Argos last won in 2012, but no disrespect to the CFL, although it is a pretty good league, it is Canadian and it's hard to compare with American football. The Blue Jays last won the World Series in 1993, and I can't even mention the TFC without a chuckle, as they have a hard time getting a victory let alone making the playoffs. That is, until this year (2015).

When you cheer for the underdogs as I do, it relieves you of any chance of being let down and disappointed that your team has lost to a team of lesser talent (in your mind). That kind of loss can put people in an angry and upset mood, and when in large groups, people go a little overboard. Riots have ensued in large cities. Car accidents have happened when disgruntled drivers pay more attention to their loss than to their driving. Fights break out between rival fans at a sporting event and neighbouring watering holes, and for what? Remember, it is just a game. Drop the childish attitude.

There are advantages to rooting for underdogs—you won't get disappointed when they lose, and when they do win, you will be elated and happy, not only because you chose the victorious team but because of how that team must feel. It's like David conquering Goliath. Not to mention that you can rub it in to the losers around you (as long as they are friends; if not, I wouldn't advise it).

Those who frequent gambling outlets have told me that wagering on teams that are not favourites to win or have only a slim chance can make you money. I am not a gambling man, so I don't know how true that is. I guess it has something to do with the odds and the amount wagered. Why does the expression "Know your limit, play within it" come to mind?

# H

Help at Any Time
Hi to Real Bank People

# Help at Any Time

This is not quite the same as donating your time, although it is related to some extent. Small gestures mean a lot to others, even though you think they are no big deal. You could help someone out who may be in a hurry, or is in an awkward situation, or is lost.

One winter day, I was getting gas at a local station. Snow was coming down and the roads were all slushy, which meant there was a good chance that salt had been applied. Cars looked like they had been doused in a mixture of dirt and white paint, and it was difficult to see out through our windshields. I had finished pumping my gas and noticed a lady at the next island just beginning to put gas in. Her vehicle was really badly covered with salt and dirt, so I took it upon myself to clean the windshield and headlights. This really took her by surprise. As I put the squeegee back, she told me my effort was greatly appreciated and thanked me with a sincere smile. A gesture like that makes you feel great, and all it took was 30 seconds.

In the past, I have helped change a flat tire for elderly people, opened doors to help those carrying bags, given directions to those who seemed to be lost, and given up a seat on a bus or subway to someone who looked tired. A small gesture on my behalf, but a big one to others. I do this not for recognition but because it makes me feel good to help. I believe that we too often forget the little things in life that make a difference.

# Hi to Real Bank People

I understand that advances in technology, and computers in particular, in most cases make life a lot easier and more convenient—especially in the banking sector. Online banking, telephone banking and as I write this cellphone banking (where you photograph a cheque, send it to your banking institution via cellphone, and voilà! instant deposit) are simply remarkable and truly ingenious.

The downside is that our society has become less social than ever. Is it our hectic and stressful lifestyle or work style that has made us all seem to forget the one important factor we are missing: communication with a live person? People who constantly take shortcuts will say it's more convenient or they just don't have the time. To be perfectly honest, I will say that for the most part people are just plan lazy. End of story!

Have you seen the bank drive-throughs lately? Are you trying to tell me that waiting in your car for a few minutes to pull out some money from the ATM is faster and more convenient than actually parking your vehicle and physically walking into the bank? I don't think so. I have parked my car, walked in and come back out with money in hand and have seen the same cars waiting in line as when I went in.

As for the bank, I would much rather walk into the building and physically see and talk to a live person for a few minutes than stick an envelope into a metal box and hope that it doesn't get lost somewhere or that my card isn't being scanned or copied by an inconspicuous camera set up by a crook to steal from me later. My father would say something like, "I don't like ATM machines because they always show me a happy face with a huge smile with the words *Have a nice day*." He would respond to the machine, "How do you know what kind of day I'm having?" It's something to think about!

# I

Instructions Should Be Read

# Instructions Should Be Read

When it comes to instructions, my friend Yasu says he likes the challenge of winging it. I would agree with him for the most part, but when you get older, patience gets thinner, and that patience will be put to a serious test sooner rather than later. In the garage right now, waiting for me, are not one but two garage-door openers, which I find a little intimidating to say the least. Let's see how this unfolds in the spring. Perhaps they will both be up before the winter sets in again. Time will tell.

Although I'm not one to brag, I have managed to do the following with little or no difficulty:

- changing tires
- changing oil and filter
- attaching a microwave to the wall
- mounting a 60-pound mirror/frame to the wall (drywall only)
- finishing a basement (except messing around with electricity and plumbing)
- building a backyard fort
- installing shelves and cabinets
- putting together coffee tables
- fishing a screwdriver through an electric baseboard heater to take out the screw with the power on (should have turned it off—I ended up 15 feet across the room with a useless screwdriver that had melted)
- finding out the hard way to wear shoes while working with a hammer and nails after successfully installing framework in the ceiling ready for drywall, jumping down from a stool onto what I thought was the basement floor and landing a piece of wood with—guess what—not one but two nails protruding. They ended up going through my foot. Not a pretty sight.

I do read the instructions for the most part; maybe I should read a safety-procedure manual as well.

# J

Jot Down Words
Just Because

# Jot Down Words

Every once in a while, I hear or see a word and wonder, *What is that?* Every day is a learning experience for the taking, and new words are certainly a part of that. Whether it's figuring out how to pronounce the word, spell the word, or understand what the word means, learning new words is a good way to pass the time when you start to get a little bored with the day's workload or would just like to learn something different. These words or sometimes phrases come in handy when you least expect it, and that's why you will always find me with a pen and paper close by wherever I go.

After a little investigative research, I discovered the following: There are approximately 1,025,109.8 (decimal ?) words in the English language (based on an estimate dated January 1st, 2014 by GLM). The global language monitor or GLM was founded in Silicon Valley in 2003 by Paul J.J. Payack which studies the world of Big Data. Another estimate was done by David Crystal (a linguist and world-renown expert on the English language) who has come up with the following summary:

- a person starting school: 500 - 600 words
- a person without formal education: 35,000 words
- a high school educated person: 50,000 words
- a college education person: 50,000 – 75,000 words

I also discovered another interesting fact and that being that Dr. Stanley Coren (an expert in canine intelligence) has stated that the average dog can understand about 165 words, possibly more with training.

# Just Because

There is no rhyme or reason as to why we should do anything out of the ordinary for anybody, other than to make us feel good or put a smile on the person's face. As a society, I find that we are becoming a bunch of computerized robots, running an endless rat race just to survive. The only time we stop is to upgrade or update ourselves with the latest technology in order to compete or outdo each other in the dog-eat-dog world. We get washed, get dressed, gulp down breakfast, get the kids off to school, fight traffic to get to work, work our derrière off to accomplish whatever it is that has to be done, fight traffic to go home, eat supper, tuck the kids into bed, wash, get ready for bed and sleep in order to do it all over again the next day.

We do this over and over without the slightest idea of what is going on beside, behind and in front of us. It's like a horse race at times. The only thing that is different is that as humans, we are not wearing visible blinders like racehorses do. We may as well wear blinders, though, as we are only focused on one thing, and that is to survive the day.

Wouldn't it be nice to stop for a moment and recognize what is going on, whether it is the driver beside you, your co-workers and their thoughts, the person behind the counter where you buy your daily coffee or your neighbour you haven't spoken to since the last discussion of indifferent weather (and that could be months ago)? Why not look at the driver beside you, and if he or she glances your way, share a smile or a short wave that could be construed as a meaning "Have a great day," instead of staring because in your mind that individual is not the best driver in the world. Do it because you want to share your happy feeling.

Co-workers, I find, are very important—you spend at least half your day with them (or a third if you count your sleep time). Your relationship with your co-workers should be healthy and positive. Share stories of home, exchange a few jokes or recipes, plan a few outings, celebrate a few birthdays.

My personal rewarding thing to do is bring in poinsettias at Christmas to the ladies in my office. It is just my way of saying thanks for the past year and wishing all the best to them and their families during the festive season. They have all helped me at one time or another during the year with a joke, a hello, a smile, concern for my well-being or help with a work-related problem, such as helping me when the copier won't work or finding me a stapler that is capable of stapling drawings together without mangling the paper. They help because they want to, not because they have to, and in case I haven't mentioned it enough, I say thank you to each and every one of them.

People behind a counter at places like Tim Horton's or McDonald's work so hard. A pleasant and meaningful thank you or an appreciative comment means so much to them. It may also give you a beneficial edge in a place where you are a regular customer, such as a little faster service next time.

Try doing one of following, just because:

- Compliment your neighbours on how green their yard looks or how clean their car is.
- Comment to total strangers on the street or in the mall about how sharply they are dressed or how cute their child is.
- Bring home flowers to your significant other every once in a while for no apparent reason—no guilt trip, no apologies, no favours, just a desire to make the day brighter for the one you love. Even though you're not looking for anything in return, you may get a surprise yourself when you least expect it. As they say, you get what you give.

While you're at it, just because, why not take a moment and start singing a song or at least humming one to yourself? Music is a beautiful and magical gift that brings people together. Anyone can join in.

Or pick up a musical instrument. You may even discover a hidden talent that you did not even know existed.

I talk in a little more detail about musical instruments in Play An Instrument.

The same could be said about picking up a paint brush and showing another hidden talent by painting a picture. A great pass time, and if others do not like what you have created just remember the old saying that goes Beauty is in the eyes of the beholder.

But you do not need an audience to enjoy music or art. Do it for you. Just because.

# K

Keep a Snack Handy
Keep a Stamp Handy

# Keep a Snack Handy

Since I've been on the go since age 13—rushing to get to school, going to work at one job and then rushing off to another, or going to play a game on the field or on the ice—there was never much time to prepare proper foods and achieve daily requirements that give a person energy to maintain a healthy lifestyle and get through the day.

Personally, for me, a normal day would mean leaving the house before six o'clock in the morning and not returning until past ten at night. Buying fast food was not an option for me, as I had to pay my own way and money back then was hard to come by. There were no funds for privileges and fun stuff, so I would muster up when I could and put snacks aside whenever possible. That meant picking up crackers, small buns and juice packs whenever they were on sale and finding a way to hide them, as things disappeared when I was staying at rooming houses and hostels while going to school. That's where I learned the importance of having a quick snack between venues, when travelling on the TTC to and from activities. It didn't matter what type of snack it was.

These snacks, although not much in terms of nutrition, helped keep me going from day to day. That is why little treats can now be found at my desk, in the glove compartment of both my cars and in my backpack when I venture outdoors. I haven't checked recently, but there are probably crackers in my golf bag somewhere. I just hope I didn't leave anything chocolate there like a candy bar, or even worse, anything perishable. Probably I should check that out.

The good thing about putting snacks away is a tendency to forget about them, and then, when you least expect it, there is something to enjoy. My long-time friend Kwan (now deceased) always had a minimart in his office desk that was full of good stuff, and he was always willing to share. That is, until the inventory seemed to disappear a lot faster than he could remember, especially after he would leave the room for a few minutes. He wouldn't get upset, as that was not his style. He simply resolved the disappearing-snack issue by locking his desk. As Kwan would say, "End of story."

# Keep a Stamp Handy

I know, I know, the stamp will soon become a thing of the past, but I still keep one or two handy just in case I decide that I want to write—that's right, not text or type but *write*—a letter or a note. Sure, you can email, text or make a phone call, but I find the good old-fashioned way to be rewarding to both the sender and the recipient. A stamp does the trick.

There have been times when, for whatever reason, a bill cannot be paid by phone or online, and therefore a stamp comes in handy. Otherwise you would have to walk or drive to pay in person before the due date. There's always time to mail a bill.

I have a tendency to put a bill aside for a bit, knowing I can do my online banking or phone banking close to a due date, and wouldn't you know it, I have either forgotten to pay or actually misplaced the statement. Please, I do not need a reminder that I can postdate a payment by phone or by online banking. I may be getting old, but I'm not that senile yet.

# L

Let a Car in Your Lane
Listen With Your Ears First
Long Drive to Work
Look on the Bright Side

# Let a Car in Your Lane

Even though I consider myself to be an experienced and confident driver, it can be a little nerve-racking and downright frustrating to try to enter a busy street from a plaza or even merge from an on-ramp onto one of the lanes on a highway. As a rule of thumb so you don't get the finger, be a little courteous and let a fellow driver in. It doesn't cost you anything, and it makes your day a little better to know you've aided another driver. You may even get a wave of thanks, which beats the finger of profanity any time of the day. While driving in Scotland a few years back, I was given the horn, as it is more than a courtesy to let someone on the highway from an on-ramp- it's the law, so I was told.

Closer to home, many a time I have seen a car pull up behind another vehicle, knowing full well that it's not going anywhere any faster, just to impede a driver who is trying to enter the roadway, and for what? Maybe, just maybe if we were a little more cautious and showed a little more courtesy while behind the wheel, we could reduce a lot of temper, frustration and road rage. The roads are for everyone's use, so let's work together.

# Listen With Your Ears First

After I was separated in 1999, I used to visit a restaurant that is no longer around today: JJ Muggs in the Woodbine Centre shopping centre at Highway 27 and Rexdale Boulevard. One night, I struck up a conversation with a young waiter who said he was glad that he could share a little of what he was doing outside of work. His dream and passion was acting, but his parents were against it, telling him that he couldn't make money that way to raise a family. I didn't want to go against his parents, since I was a parent myself, but I did mention that he should follow his dream and try his passion for the theatre on a small scale, using it as a hobby but keeping his focus on the reality that only a very small percentage of people who want to act make it to the big time. The rest fail with no other plans. I mentioned that he should concentrate on another career and actually helped him understand what he was up against.

The next time I went to JJ Muggs, I was with someone for the first time since my separation, with no motive other than enjoying dinner with another human being for a change after volunteering at the condo to set up a Halloween party for the young people in the building. This young man was our waiter that night, and out of the blue he sat down for a moment and said something like, "I just wanted to thank you for your friendly, not judgmental words." He had talked with his parents and worked out a game plan for his future. He would go to Humber College for his main education and continue to enjoy doing stand-up at a couple of comedy clubs and bars on the weekend to test his skills, knowing full well that it might not be his future. If nothing else, he would be able to enjoy himself for a while.

It was a win-win situation, especially since I got brownie points with my dinner companion without even trying. It will make you feel good to be open-minded and lend an ear to someone who is looking to speak. Be willing to listen. I like to think I made a difference that night. He sure thought so.

# Long Drive to Work

I listen to my favourite radio station, 680AM, not only for up-to-date news, weather and sports but also for traffic reports so as I know how much earlier I have to leave due to accident or construction, or whether I should plan a different route to avoid the tie-up altogether.

Regardless of the circumstances and duration, your daily drive should be a time to forget about everything you have just left and all that lies in store for you at your destination. Sit back, concentrate on driving and enjoy the ride. Engage in some reflection. Think of a pleasant event you've enjoyed or are planning. Look forward to another great golf day with your friends or your next vacation. These thoughts should make your drive more enjoyable. Listen to music and, if not embarrassed by your passengers, sing to the music with gusto, almost as if you are the actual performer of the moment.

Our heads need that break from the everyday monotonous, tedious, stressful routine. Worrying about it all the time is not doing you any good. Let it go and enjoy the moment. Just think: there are no calls to interrupt you, no one breathing down your neck for work-related problems and deadlines, no children to worry about, no bills to pay, no in-laws to hound you. It's a time to sit, relax and reflect in any way you want.

My drive from home to the office is approximately forty minutes each way, and every moment is peaceful and serene, with nothing but music or laughter (funny 820AM) for my ears and nothing but horses, cows, farms and trees for my eyes. I find that scenario very pleasing. No matter the distance, sit back and enjoy.

For those who complain about travelling to work and the length of time to get back and forth, I have a simple solution: move closer to work or work closer to home. It's your choice, not the fault of others.

I have at times been frustrated with the duration of my drive to work due to problems beyond my control, and by listening to music or a bit of comedy helps me forget about the frustration and most of the extra time required to get where I want to go. It's just not worth it. To you or the drivers around you.

# Look on the Bright Side

The adage in the title for this page has been around since the beginning of time or as long as I can remember, which seem at times to be one and the same. Putting it very simply, we as human beings have a knack for finding the negative in everything that affects our lives at one point or another. To get yourself looking on the bright side, put yourself in the following scenarios for a moment and think about how you would react and respond. These examples are from my past and may not be ones that you can relate to, but they're worth pondering nonetheless:

| Event | Feelings at the Time | Looking on the Bright Side |
|---|---|---|
| Failed job interview | Disappointment, depression, self-pity | Getting so close to an opportunity gave me drive. Opportunities and perseverance do eventually pay off. |
| Stuck in traffic behind an accident | Anger and frustration | Seeing ambulances and fire trucks made me think, *I am not in the accident, dead or injured,* and that made me appreciate my situation. |
| Left alone as a young teen (hard to let go of this one) | Hurt, anger, worry, anxiety, fear | This experience made me a stronger person and totally independent. It forced me to make good life decisions and choices. |

| Failed marriage | Disappointment and deflation | The end of my marriage forced me to acknowledge my faults and seek ways to become a better person. |
| --- | --- | --- |
| Severe injury ended my hockey dream at age 17 | Devastation and anger | I gained the determination and mindset to fight back and stop feeling sorry for myself. Self-pity did not defeat me, and I became a stronger person |
| Health issues | Fear, worry, sadness | Being sick made me appreciate life and enjoy it while I was able. I knew I would be able to walk out of the hospital after. |

In short, the grass is not always greener on the other side. It could be mould for all you know! Be thankful for all you have and for all that you can do. Things could be a heck of a lot worse.

# M

Movies on Sale for Later

# Movies on Sale for Later

How many nights or rainy days have you thought about doing nothing or just lounging around, either reading a book, listening to music or watching a movie? It's not like we make time for ourselves very often. When it happens, the last thing you should be worrying about is what to do with this free time. It could be an hour, two hours or, dare I say, a whole afternoon or evening.

That's why in one of my bedrooms, now a TV room, you will find a collection of movies, puzzle books, CDs and even a PS3 in case I get the urge to show myself how old I am by playing video games. Regarding the movies, heck, I don't even know what I have to watch, for the most part. Living by Albion Mall in Etobicoke for a few years meant shopping at a No Frills Food Store, and while trying to avoid the mishaps of shopping carts and the free-flying elbows of shoppers fighting for specials, I noticed a bin full of movies. There were some black-and-white films from a long time ago, some comedies, a few action movies and even a few cartoons.

Maybe after I complete this little book, I will make the time to actually watch them. But what I'm trying to say is you don't have to be too picky when you come across these inexpensive little gems. Just take a quick peek to make sure they're English. The last thing you need is to get comfortable with a nice cup of tea and a few snacks, hit the remote and have to read English subtitles. Very frustrating.

# N

Never Drink
Never Take Play Too Seriously
Never Refuse a Hug
Never Take Others for Granted
Never Be Too Proud to Ask for Help
Never Yell in Public
Nurses Are the Best

# Never Drink

By "never drink," I mean never drink in excess to be social; be social so that you never have to drink in excess. It's unfair and unjust to criticize people who drink in moderation while attending a function, a celebration or a sporting event. The problem for me is that some people get a little carried away, especially if there is an open bar or the seventh inning of a ball game (last inning to serve beer) is near. That is when those who feel they have to hoard all they can carry come back to their seats with at least one beer in each hand, just to make sure they aren't left out or to top off their quota for the day. It's not like there is going to be shortage tomorrow.

It's an addiction. A prominent politician has stated many times that he's not an addict, but how many times has he made a complete jackass of himself in public and then denied his problem? Unfortunately, my family (certain ones close to me while growing up as a child) was all too familiar with that form of activity. I will not go into details, but what I saw growing up is the main reason I do not indulge in that lifestyle. I saw too much excessiveness and how it affects those close by.

A glass of wine at Christmas or New Year's with family or friends, or a beer at a birthday or a BBQ—those are the extent of my consumption. To be quite honest, like most of my friends, I can be silly without indulging in spirits. The good thing is I will not regret it the next day as I suffer a hangover.

# Never Take Play Too Seriously

Why is it that when an individual of the male gender of the human species decides to play a game—checkers, cards, video games, golf, hockey, whatever—he turns it into a competition as if there is something to achieve by winning at all costs? Other than bragging rights with friends, there's no reason to play with a competitive chip on your shoulder. It's called a game because it's intended for fun and enjoyment. The only goal for me personally is to improve my own game. If you have to beat something, why not your previous outing? That should be satisfaction in itself.

All too often when people do not do well at a game, they are seen to do one of the following:

- get mad and frustrated
- get depressed
- yell out loud
- blame it on something other than their lack of skill
- throw their clubs (if golf), bat (if baseball), stick (if hockey), bike (if cycling)
- break or damage something (hopefully their own stuff)
- hit someone

To these people, I have to be the bearer of bad news. I can guarantee that everyone around you loses all respect for you and may think twice about joining you next time. That is what you really should worry about—not your game but your friends. That is what is important, not winning. In fact, when you get angry and frustrated, whether they admit it or not, those around you want you to mess up even more. It's frustrating for them to be around you when you're in a rotten mood.

Do what I tell my children: "If you are not getting paid to play, do not take it seriously." Play to have fun and do your best. The winning part is being with friends and family, enjoying the game and bonding with each other.

# Never Refuse a Hug

It may be a little peculiar, but I find a warm and meaningful hug extremely gratifying, whether it's from my spouse, a friend or one of my children, grandchildren, nephews or nieces. It shows a true and meaningful expression of gratitude, forgiveness, happiness, I'm here for you, condolence, etc.

The gesture to me shows how much someone really cares, and the expression is true and sincere, with feeling put into it. The same could be said for a handshake or a high five, but those are more common among men. How many times do you see guys hug each other after a goal at a hockey game or a grand slam in a baseball game?

But one must beware of the handshake that does not have a good tight grip, so to speak. That means it is a forced shake, and you should be a little wary of the person behind it. There is either a motive or some other reason why someone would show the kind of handshake that is not real, not true. This is coming from life experience.

# Never Take Others for Granted

"Never take for granted." Four simple words that really don't stand out individually, but put them together and they have a powerful message for you. That message applies to almost everything you do on a daily basis.

In any relationship, the number-one piece of excellent advice is to never take the other person for granted. Relationships are special and should not be forgotten over time. Remember to do the little things on an ongoing basis that brought the two of you together in the first place. You can never put too much spice in a relationship. When you add the surprise factor, it could be downright magical.

A good friend should never be taken for granted. This is a person who is there with you through the good times, bad times, in sickness and health—almost like a marriage, come to think of it. A friend will not pass judgment on you, right or wrong, and will be there by your side at a moment's notice.

That kind of friendship is rare, and I am fortunate to have it in my life. Yasu has been close by for over forty-five years now, and our friendship is still going strong. I disappeared from our relationship for a few years out of selfishness, but wouldn't you know it, neither a judgment nor a scolding was passed to me from him when the ordeal was over. He went through some tough times himself during that period, and although I felt guilty for not being there for him, Yasu showed me nothing but forgiveness. To this day, I am humbled and blessed by our friendship and will never again take it for granted.

It's a little different, but your work is also a place where you should never take people for granted. You may think that after years of effort to get where you are now, you have a right to slack off and lay back and reap the financial rewards and freedom you are accustomed to, but your work ethic should never change. In fact, it should be refreshed and fine-tuned from time to time. Two things to think about: people around you notice good work ethic and bad work ethic, and some of those people are higher up on the food chain than you. At most workplaces, you are just a number, and believe it or not, you can be replaced. Don't give anyone ammunition to do so.

The environment should also not be taken for granted. If we keep abusing it, there will be serious consequences for our children and grandchildren to deal with and live with. You can tell it's beginning because of all the floods, tsunamis, hurricanes, earthquakes and tornadoes. Mother Nature is trying to tell us something. Let's listen before it's too late.

# Never Be Too Proud to Ask for Help

This one is mainly for the male readers. Let me explain why.

How many times have you seen a male driving in circles looking for a place he cannot find—in other words, lost. You may see him walking up and down aisles in a department store trying to find a particular item, or holding a couple of items in his hands trying to find out which one is better and which one is on sale, or always using and depending on GPS while driving. I know, as I have been there, but you know what? I have learned to accept the fact that from time to time, I need help finding something. And so I ask.

It makes life a lot easier when you ask. You will be surprised how happy people are to help when you are friendly and courteous. Drop the ego and ask for help.

# Never Yell in Public

Yelling or raising your voice in a public place—like a mall, a restaurant, a sporting event or even an office—seems to be considered acceptable these days. It could be a parent scolding a child, a disagreement that becomes a full-blown heated argument, an employer blaming an employee for a costly mistake, or an unruly sports fan railing against another fan for whatever reason. Regardless of who is right or who is wrong, such differences of opinion should be aired behind closed doors, not in such a way that strangers can't avoid hearing about it.

It can be downright humiliating and embarrassing to be singled out and placed on the receiving end of insults, accusations and blame. It would be so simple and diplomatic to discuss the problem in a reasonable tone of voice in a private setting without people around taking in the circus. Regardless of the outcome, such a scene can leave a scar on both parties. One will have to live with a reputation for being an egotistical bully that will be hard to get rid of, while the other has to live with the reputation of being the weak one with not much bite in his or her bark. Both lose the respect of those forced to witness the incident first-hand.

# Nurses Are the Best

From what I can remember, it was around Grade 6 or 7 that I had my first trip in an ambulance after nearly drowning while on a school trip to a public pool. My last trip was approximately four or five years ago while attempting to go to the office after shovelling snow. I did not make it to work and was picked up in a parking lot in Etobicoke (something about my heart, but all's well that ends well). I lost count of the number of times in between the first and the last trip; there have been a couple of trips by ambulance and countless times friends have driven me. On top of that, when you have children, it is a sure bet that you will be there a few times while they are growing up. My four were no exception.

While waiting to be looked at, whether at triage, registration, the waiting room or an inside cubicle (amidst what I call the war zone), there is a sense of constant organized chaos. This goes on 24-7, not nine to five. Nurses see it all, from bleeding noses to broken bones to heart attacks to gunshot and stab wounds to drug overdoses. All of these are bad enough on their own, but when a child is involved, I have no clue what they must go through emotionally. I know that they are well-trained, caring professionals who have to keep it together, but there are times when they must feel hopeless knowing the situation is way beyond their control. They see and have to deal with different life-altering issues on a daily basis, but what happens after the shift is over?

Work stress can stay with you long after a shift is complete. I am sure it must play havoc with nurses' personal lives. Most of us could not handle the day-to-day stress that they have to go through. Add to that the abuse they have to put up with from inconsiderate patients ranting and doctors' constant demands, and it should put them over the edge—but it doesn't. If it were me, I can guarantee you that I would be fired for refusing to work for unruly doctors and uncooperative and inconsiderate patients. There would be attempted murder charges if I had to put up with that nonsense for too long.

I salute nurses for their dedication and professionalism, and for the care that I and my family have received over the years and will never take for granted. I have so much respect for nurses. Thank you!

Out-of-the-Box Return

# Out-of-the-Box Return

You receive an item in a box, nicely packaged, taped throughout, protected by all shapes and sizes of Styrofoam, accompanied by booklets and instructions taped in plastic—only to discover after tearing it all open that the item was not what you were expecting or did not work, or parts were missing. Now it has to be returned.

I don't know about you, but I have a difficult time trying to put everything that came out of that box back into that box just the way it was when it first arrived. There are pieces of Styrofoam left over that won't fit unless broken up a bit and pushed in hard enough to make the box bulge. I even have trouble sliding the booklets in at the very end and then taping the box together. It's no wonder some stores give us a funny look or refuse to take the item back in some instances. Often the items look like shredded wheat when returned.

I'm trying now to take items out of a box in reverse sequence to the way I'd have to put them back in—trying to think like an engineer in reverse. I try to memorize what the contents look like when I first open the lid; if I remember, I'll take a couple of pictures which should give me an idea of how the puzzle works. It doesn't always help, but I'll try anything so as not to embarrass myself when I return the item.

# P

Parked Car—Remember
Pass Time While in Traffic
Pen, Pencil and Paper
People at Work
Phone Out of the Blue
Pictures on Hand
Play an Instrument
Poppy Problem Solved
Pops and Maple Leaf Gardens
Print Pictures Later
Put Change Away

# Parked Car—Remember

It's tough for me to admit, but to be quite honest, I've failed to remember where I parked my car on a few occasions over the years, with consequences ranging from laughter to panic.

Yorkdale Shopping Centre is very large and quite popular, and it is very hard to find parking at the best of times. Sometimes, you have to park so far away, you would almost think that a shuttle service would be beneficial. There are also times when, in a hurry, you take whatever spot you find and hastily leave your car to run into the mall without realizing where you are situated. Walking up and down aisles of numerous vehicles, bags in hand, clicking your car alarm becomes an exercise in futility, not to mention an embarrassment.

Scarborough Town Centre (I think) can also be a little adventurous if you're not careful. One of my most memorable lost-car incidents happened here. I had borrowed a friend's car to go pick up an item at the mall and, in my haste and inattentiveness, had not paid attention to where I parked it. When I came out, I made a beeline straight towards where the car should have been, and guess what? It was not there. All I saw was a little garbage on a vacant parking spot.

Sure of my surroundings, I quickly summoned the security team in the mall and explained the circumstances, coming to the conclusion that my friend's car had been stolen ... only to have it pointed out to me a few minutes later that the car was actually parked around the corner on the other side of the store on a lower level. You see, I had inadvertently come out the wrong door on a different level without paying attention. Talk about embarrassing. I asked security how they found the car so fast, and with a smile I was told that this happens more often than you'd think. It didn't make me feel any better.

Another embarrassing moment came in the spring of 2013 when I was attending my daughter's graduation ceremony from OCAD University, which was being held at Roy Thompson Hall. Parking downtown is at a premium. Not only is it virtually impossible to find a spot, but when you do, it can cost you an arm and a leg. You need to plan on an hour of aggravation before finding a spot. That day, I didn't have an hour, and so I ended up parking half a dozen streets west of Roy Thompson Hall. I had to run to make it on time, and I didn't stop to take notice of exactly where I parked.

After the ceremony, we headed in the direction of where I thought I was parked. To my dismay, not only could I not remember the lot, but I also couldn't remember the street it was on. Suddenly, it was panic time. It's one thing to lose a car in a parking lot and walk around until you find it. It's another to forget entirely in a busy and chaotic atmosphere. After some anxious moments and careful thinking, we did manage to find my car. On a brighter note, it was a wonderful ceremony, and I don't think there was anything that could have made me as a parent more proud than seeing my child grow up to be a remarkable young adult.

By opening up about my mistakes, I hope to make people more aware of their surroundings so an enjoyable day doesn't turn into a nightmare. We do not need to add any more stress to our day. This is why, whenever I go anywhere, I always try to see where I have parked—and by that I mean landmarks like light poles, parking-aisle designations (if applicable) and entrances to the mall in relation to the parking aisle so as to take the same way back. With airport parking, it is a good idea to write down not only the level but the parking section on that level, which is found on neighbouring columns. I made the mistake once of taking the wrong ramp from the terminal to the parking deck. Although I had the right spot, I was 10 feet too high on the next level.

As far as downtown parking goes, take the TTC. If you must park down there, I advise you to write down not only the name of the parking lot or garage with your exact spot but maybe the names of a few streets and businesses surrounding the lot. It may seem to be a silly exercise, but it could save you some time and frustration. I know it has saved me on more than one occasion.

# Pass Time While in Traffic

Whether it involves an accident up ahead, malfunctioning traffic lights or road construction, getting caught in traffic is a fact of life for drivers. We have all been in that frustrating situation at one time or another. After years of joining the irate motorists who are cursing and swearing, getting hot under the collar, losing their temper, yelling out loud, pounding the horn, smacking the window and otherwise expressing their outrage, I finally came to the conclusion that hey, there's nothing I can do about it.

When you think about it, what kind of an example are we setting? If our children hear or see what we are doing behind the wheel, "monkey see, monkey do," as the old adage goes.

Try a different approach. If you're by yourself in that traffic, turn this disruptive portion of your drive into a game. Especially if you are in a traffic jam with cars all around, try making words out of letters of the licence plates, or expand the letters into words by adding a letter here and there. You would be surprised how much of a stress release this can be—and if there are children in the car, it can be particularly fun. You could even use the numbers for math practice.

It's not worth it to get frustrated for nothing, especially since there is nothing you can do to resolve the issue. Just have fun killing time. Remember, it could be worse—you could be the one in the accident up ahead. Count your blessings.

# Pen, Pencil and Paper

This may be outdated, but I will remind everyone that I am from the old school. I know that smartphones, Blackberries, iPods and all of that can be handy for keeping track of appointments, store locations, cost of items, places of interest and so many other purposes. For me, however, a pencil or pen and paper are much more handy and convenient while driving, especially when there is another person in the car.

In my car, I have a small pad with a pencil in my glove compartment. When I see an interesting sign, store or even phone number on a billboard that could benefit me or someone close to me, it's easy to pull over safely if by myself to jot the information down quickly and carry on to where I am going, or to have my passenger note it for me.

When you get a little older, whether you want to admit it or not, the memory slips, and information must be written down, as it all can no longer be memorized—especially by the male brain. We all need a little help from time to time.

Let me clarify that if you are by yourself driving and a thought comes to you, no matter how important, please do pull over to the side safely, stop the car and do what you have to do at the moment. I do not condone texting, talking on a cellphone, reading or doing anything that could distract you for any period of time while behind the wheel. You must be totally focused, with both hands on the wheel. If not, you are inconsiderate and stupid, with no concern for the well-being of yourself and others.

# People at Work

People do not realize this, but you spend more time with your co-workers than you do with your partner on any given day, as mentioned earlier in "Just Because." Think about it: eight hours a day at work is 33 percent of a day, plus breaks (lunch); if you take into consideration texts, emails and phone conversations, that percentage is even higher. If you work different shifts, like police, paramedics, doctors and factory workers do, then it may become 50 percent or more.

That's why it's so important to develop a healthy relationship with your co-workers. When someone during your work time ticks you off, it's easy to bring that anger, disappointment and frustrated attitude home. What should be a healthy, loving and happy home life then becomes damaged by your bad day at the office. It's hard to say openly, but to be honest, I have come home more times than I would like to remember with a chip on my shoulder, and it's not a healthy time for anyone involved.

Although periodically I still come home in not such a good mood, I will say those days are now few and far between. When they happen, I share them with someone close. When you share a not-so-good day with someone special, the healing process begins. Let me tell you, it's no fun sleeping on the couch alone. That has to be a big deterrent to bringing your work home.

You would be surprised how fast, enjoyable and even productive a day can be when you have a positive attitude towards work. You don't have to be at your desk for eight hours with blinders on and earplugs in. Take a little time to get to know your co-workers, exchange a few jokes, tell some family tales, share a coffee break and have lunch together from time to time. Obviously, you are not going to take too long of a break; the boss may not be happy with that. But I'm quite sure it's okay from time to time to bond with workers a little, which can be productive and motivating. That's something the boss should be happy about.

It is no fun to work in a toxic environment. If that's how you feel, it's time for a change! I must let you know about the people I have met over the past 44 years in the construction business. Most of these people have had an influence on my life and the way I look at not only work but life in general. Every day is a learning process, and being in an office or any workplace is no different.

I am only going to mention people who have had a real positive influence on my life. There are a few who have been unfairly critical, but I do not like to publicly call out anyone in particular. As the old adage goes, "If you have nothing nice to say about someone, then say nothing." That saying is particular true because there are always two sides to a story, and yours may not always be the right one.

## Gary Hill

Although Gary was my first boss (I was hired by Canadian Patent Scaffolding back in 1970 as a draftsman), it soon became evident that he was more than just a boss. At the time, I was putting pressure on myself to produce and produce quickly, not only to fit in but also because I wanted to stay. Gary saw that and helped me not only in the workplace but outside in the real world as well.

We often had to work overtime to meet deadlines, and to show his appreciation, Gary always made sure there was pizza, beer and conversation afterwards to help us relax and unwind. He did this not because he had to, but because he wanted to. On late nights, he would make sure I got home, as a car was not an option for me financially at the time. It was bus, subway, streetcar and a walk to get to work. He was a caring and compassionate person.

There was always some sort of activity going on, and Gary was right there organizing, helping set up, participating or making sure that people got there on time as well as home after. I will always remember the lunch hours when Gary, Gibson, Mike and myself would walk down to the park at Fort York and throw a football around. In reality, I believe Gary was trying to fit in, not the other way around. To be honest, although I never mentioned it to him, I considered him to be my mentor, and I am thankful that he gave me a chance.

## Bob Dean

Bob was a true gentleman in every sense of the word. Although I was only at Ontario Formwork for approximately one and a half years, it was where I was working when I got married. Bob would give me advice and talks similar to what a father does for a son. His family devotion, compassion, love and morals are what I learned from him and practice to this day.

He also taught me that when golfing, I should use a five iron to put the ball on the green from the fairway instead of a pitching wedge. A little different from the norm, but I still use the obscure technique today. It works for me (most of the time).

## Ken Watkins

When you work alongside a person for a quarter of a century, you get to know a little about him. With Ken, there were talks, sometimes about nothing, but for the most part there was always something to take away from our morning rituals. He was a dedicated worker who gave his all, so to speak, to help Avenue Structures prosper, and he's a big factor in how the company operates today.

The only thing more important to Ken than work was—and still is—his family. His dedication to and compassion for his family was always first and foremost. They were his biggest priority in life. Our talks were mainly regarding children and the ups and downs of family life. Ken had reinforced the morals of being a good parent, and it was evident when he spoke. You could see how proud he was of his family, and when I had a chance to talk to him briefly at a golf tournament this past summer, his children and grandchildren were still at the top of his list. It is so nice to have the privilege of knowing someone of his stature and love for his family after all these years.

If you ask my first two sons, Jason and Nicholas, about Ken, I can guarantee you that the first thing that comes to mind is the chocolate man. When Ken would visit my house he always brought chocolate donuts for my sons. We agreed to have lunch soon after the golfing, and I hope I have the chance to catch up with him before this comes out.

## Alice Z.

I have been privileged to know Alice since my first days with Hardrock Forming back in August 2001, and up until the present I can honestly say that she has had a positive influence on me. Whether it is her work ethic, her love and concern for her family or her warm and caring personality, I have the utmost respect for her. I have always found Alice to be attentive and very understanding in our conversations. She's a very honest and sincere person, never judgmental—truly one of a kind!

## Michael N.

Although I had known Michael for quite a while before with Hardrock Forming, it wasn't until I joined the company that I actually understood what kind of a person he was. Over the years of working with him, he was not just a co-worker but also a close friend. The conversations we have had along with the stories we have shared have shown me that being strong yet humble works. I know that my day is always going to be better after our early morning discussions. It is a privilege to call Michael my friend, and the friendship will never be taken for granted.

## Others who have inspired me

As I mention the people who have influenced me and made me a better person who truly enjoys going to the workplace, it would not be fair to leave out the others I work with who also inspire me and make my day a better one. They include Mirka, Connie, Nola, Ela (who has a great sense of humour and a smile that would light up any room), Alissa, Aldo (good storyteller with a very contagious laugh), Halyna, Antonietta (your favourite receptionist), Jason, Chris, Danko, George, Paul, Piero and Elena.

These are the people who help make the company a very enjoyable place to work—and work they do, creating an excellent environment that is extremely efficient and productive. Those traits are hard to find in today's world, but if anyone would like a similar environment, they should come here and take note of our well-oiled machine.

There's one more person I would like to mention: Jomar U. Although I have never had the privilege of working alongside Jomar, I have the utmost respect for him, as he has taught me so much in such a short time whenever I have visited the Philippines. I have observed him and seen a bit of his working relationship with his employees. The respect he shows his workers and concern for their well-being is reflected by the way they work and the way they produce. Jomar expects everyone to put in a full day of work but shows his appreciation through talks, parties, lunches and helping families in need when the time arises. The respect is mutual, and his employees seem to be a happy group whenever I have been there.

Jomar shared a story with me about when he first started out in the business. He would have to carry these drums (containers) of marinade for chicken from point A to point B. He had to do it by public transit—and that meant being on a crowded "jeepney" (imagine a shrunken-down bus open all around, with people riding like sardines inside and hanging around outside for a ride). At times Jomar would be asked to leave, as the odour of his container was overwhelming.

Jomar started at the bottom, so he knows a little of how hard the work can be. I find him to be very attentive and always eager to learn. The other part of Jomar that I have witnessed is his love, dedication, and compassion for his family. His family is the number-one priority in his life. You can tell by the prominent smile. In short, I can honestly say that Jomar is a strong, confident, intelligent, proud, yet very humble and sincere young man. I will humbly say to him, "Thank you Jomar for allowing me to learn so much in so little time."

I have been in the construction industry going on forty-five years at the time of writing, and of those years, approximately forty have been in estimating. The bulk of that has been in concrete, but I have dabbled in areas of masonry, excavation, reinforcing and flooring, to mention a few. I bring this up only because, just recently, a co-worker of mine who is right across the hall from my office came upon a poem that he thinks has been around for a very, very long time. He decided to share it with me. It sums up the experience of being an estimator very accurately and appropriately, and goes as follows:

## The Estimator

A construction man stood at the gate
His face was worn and old.
He meekly asked the man of fate
Admission to the fold.
"What have you done?" St. Peter asked.
"To seek permission here?"
"I was an estimator down on earth
For many a weary year."
The gate swung sharply open, then
As old Peter punched a bell,
"Come in," he said, "and take a harp.
You've had your share of hell"

—Anonymous

Note: You would have to be an estimator who has been around for quite some time in order to totally understand and appreciate this poem. I know I do.

# Phone Out of the Blue

Without any rhyme or reason, as the old saying goes, why not pick up the phone and call someone out of the blue, just to say hi or ask how the family is. Notice that I didn't say to send an email, text, tweet, Facebook post or other form of social media—so impersonal and robotic! Try it old school, and you will be honestly surprised by the reaction you receive. It's much more meaningful when a voice with emotion is heard and words are not structured before sending them via the phone, tablet or computer.

When time is limited, I understand the texting, but if you have a few spare minutes, pick up the phone—or, even more antiquated, write a few lines on a piece of paper or a card and mail it to someone. I know it means physically putting that piece of paper in an envelope, licking it to seal it, putting a stamp on the written address side of the envelope, and finding a mailbox to drop it into so it can be delivered. It seems like a lot of work to tell someone that you are thinking of him or her, but you know what? That effort is greatly appreciated by the one who receives that envelope. Whether it is an old friend, a relative who lives far away or a child, just seeing their name means a whole lot more than reading a text.

I know it sure means more to me. My daughter, Jennifer, still phones me almost every day—which always puts a smile on my face and a warm feeling in my heart—and still makes her own cards for me on special occasions. Nothing is more valuable or rewarding than receiving something personal from a loved one. It shows their character and affection.

# Pictures on Hand

As I write this little passage, I am looking at a couple of pictures on the corner of my desk that I change from time to time for a fresh look. They are always of my children, my grandchildren, my close friends or my dog. It does not matter who is there; the pictures always put a smile on my face no matter what mood I am in.

Pictures bring warmth, comfort, happiness and even a little bit of love to brighten up a day otherwise filled with sadness, boredom and stress. Everyone who is close to me knows that I have had my share of not-so-good days, and these pictures do help. No matter what your day has done or is doing to you, a little reminder of those close to you who care could make all the difference in the world in changing your day into a better one.

You could even put these pictures in your wallet—or as in the modern case, your cellphone, tablet or iPad—and that way you could be reminded of those close to you any time of day, at work or on the road. I truly believe that this will give you more of an appreciation for those close to you. I am sure you have heard of the old adage, "A picture is worth a thousand words."

# Play an Instrument

Some say that the ability to play music is a God-given gift some people are just born with, while others practice for years of endless and painstaking sacrifice in order to achieve some sort of recognition. Whether in front of a large audience with accolades and applause or in front of family and friends, it must be rewarding to the musician to see people enjoying a musical interlude. If you are talented enough, you can make some pretty good money doing what you enjoy—and if you can make a living doing what you love, even better. I am envious of musicians in that respect.

Although my father and I had numerous differences in life, I felt privileged to watch and enjoy him playing the mouth organ, otherwise known as a harmonica. Of course it was a Hohner. He was a self-taught player of this little instrument and would not think twice about pulling it out of his shirt pocket and playing songs. I don't think he realized the crowd he would attract. Around him there would be people clapping, humming, smiling, foot tapping, etc. He was in his own world and did it for his own enjoyment. Also in his repertoire was a bigger version known as a corncob mouth organ, if I am not mistaken. When he brought that out, it was like magic hearing different pitches and sounds.

Those little instruments, along with my sister Vera's accordion, have been collecting dust inside of boxes, along with a cheap keyboard I bought a few years ago after I was encouraged to take introductory piano lessons. Even though I fully intend to teach myself to play the harmonica one day, an intimidating fear of failure overcomes me from time to time. I do intend to conquer that fear and begin playing. I just hope I'll be able to appreciate the sounds before it is too late. The other reason to learn is that it would be nice to show my children and grandchildren so they may one day show interest in music and all it can do.

Playing music is a wonderful way of expressing yourself, especially if you are having fun. That's a part of life we all should do more of, and we can do it together. Even if you are not that good, make some noise and enjoy yourself. You may be pleasantly surprised.

One word of advice I would like to share is, if you are an animal lover as I am, do your pets a favour and don't let them be close to you while you're attempting to play. Their ears are extremely sensitive, and loud music can damage their eardrums. It's not fair to them and can be discouraging to you. Chelsea, my dog, makes her own painful sounds, shakes her head and then disappears when I fool around on the harmonica or keyboard.

# Poppy Problem Solved

I am a proud Canadian—one who willingly displays my appreciation by waving a flag on special days, wearing red and white, cheering at world sporting events and honouring those who helped give me the freedom and rights that I so proudly enjoy and appreciate today. That includes history from as far back as the War of 1812 to more recently with our troops in Afghanistan, and especially honouring our troops on Remembrance Day, November 11. At 11 a.m. on that special day every year—the 11th hour of the 11th day of the 11th month—I always make time for the two minutes of silence to remember the lives lost so that I and my family can enjoy all the freedoms we have today.

The one place I've always drawn the line in my patriotic appreciation is the poppy. The poppy is a very proud and honourable way of showing your appreciation for the efforts of those who helped end World War I (November 11, 1918). For years, wearing the poppy properly meant pushing a pin through some part of your shirt, blouse or jacket to hold it in place on the upper left side of your body. Sounds simple enough right?

I can't speak for others, but I have been jabbed by the longer-than-necessary pins, and I often lose part or all of the poppy before the day is done. I've tried sticking small bits of rubber from ends of pencils to hold it into place, but still no guarantee. Then, about five or six years ago, while waiting for a plane and enjoying a coffee, I saw another passenger walking by with a poppy on his jacket. He had used a Canadian patriotic lapel pin to attach the poppy. Ingenious! Not only are you showing your respect by honouring our troops, but you are also proudly displaying your patronage to Canada.

Since then, I have gone out and bought lots of these pins and given them away when I visit foreign places. Let me tell you, they are treasured very much by the receiver. Sometimes we think too hard to find a solution.

# Pops and Maple Leaf Gardens

During my teen years in the mid-1960s and early 1970s, survival for me was trying to complete my high school programme while providing for myself by taking any kind of employment I could, with one of the most notable places being the infamous Maple Leaf Gardens on Carlton Street in Toronto. There was a man who worked there who went by the name of Pops. I guess he would have been in his mid-sixties back then and maybe five foot four in height, with a body weight of around 120 pounds soaking wet.

He was such an inspiration to me, and boy could he hustle. Pops was always the first one to sign up before a game to sell whatever he would be able to sell the most of—and back then, it was pop and peanuts. The more you sold, the more you made. That's where I learned about commission. I also learned structure, self-confidence, responsibility and how to hustle to make the most. I still use some of that work ethic today. Pops didn't tell me, but all I had to do to learn was watch him do his magic.

Before I forget, it was also Pops who told me and the others to stay clear of a certain man, as Pops would tell us that the guy just didn't seem right or there was something funny about that man. For all those who have followed the news, he was a sex offender who managed to ruin young boys' lives over many years. We were lucky to get this warning and other great advice from Pops, a man who seemed to have had a hard life.

My only guilt is that I never got to know Pops, other than saying hello as we went into work, goodnight as we both went home after a game, and maybe a few words when we crossed paths during the night. There were a few opportunities for more, but neither of us could muster up the effort to sit and chat for a bit. He had such a sincere and contagious smile, and I will never forget the few words of wisdom he shared with me. Pops was a beautiful person.

# Print Pictures Later

After a party, a celebration, a vacation or a special event, it is natural to want to look at the pictures you have taken. For the most part, I am among those who can't wait to view pictures or share them with others—whether on the computer, via social networks or by physically printing pictures. Why not take a step back, though, and put them aside for a bit?

You may be pleasantly surprised if you wait a while, because you forget what is actually on the memory card. It will be like sharing pictures with yourself. I also believe that you will have a different perspective on what you see, and you will probably spend more time on other details, objects that you wouldn't notice right away. The proof to that is sitting down with a photo album that has been around for years. See how long you glance at one of those pictures compared to one recently taken.

# Put Change Away

Do you know someone who has a bad or nervous habit of playing with loose change in his pocket, or who just by walking makes an annoying sound of coins rattling together? It's as if the person is hoarding coins for whatever reason, or telling the world, "Listen to me, I have money!" It is very annoying to listen to, and for that reason alone I refuse to keep change in my pocket.

Instead, I keep my change in a little compartment in the car, so when I have a few minutes to enjoy while driving around with a McDonald's, Tim Horton's or Second Cup nearby, I can make a pit stop not only to empty (my bladder) but refill (with a cup of coffee). I always have a guilty conscience going into a place with a large bill for a small order. It's nice to have those coins on hand.

Coins also come in handy if you know that there will be an opportunity to donate to the Red Cross, Salvation Army, Boy Scouts on apple day or Air Cadets on tag day. Even when I park the car to ride the subway downtown, change is beneficial for purchasing tokens or giving to the artists and musicians hired by TTC to play music while we wait for the subway.

Just to let you know, I even used change once to purchase a lottery ticket at a local convenience store, and wouldn't you know, that ticket won $20. Who knew you could make investments with a return of 400 percent with change? Not all the time, mind you, but in this case it worked.

# Q

Quarter, Toonie and Loonie
Quotes and Expressions

# Quarter, Toonie and Loonie

Most of the time we have change in our pockets, but it seems more times than not we manage to lose it, spend it or misplace it at the times we need it most. Going to the supermarket or a large store outlet these days is bad enough for me, but when I have to deposit a coin in order to push a cart—using in most cases a quarter or a loonie—then it becomes more frustrating. That is why I try to keep at least a couple of those coins in my car so I can grab them when I go to a plaza, just in case. The problem I find is there is a tendency to use them when purchasing a coffee and or a muffin, which normally happens (you guessed it) right before I go to a store that requires a shopping cart.

It's kind of embarrassing when you stalk someone in a parking lot ready to take their buggy if it is left unattended. I have done that a few times.

If you feel generous enough, a little change—which is nothing more to you than a little noise in your pocket when you walk—can be pulled out and given to a homeless person in a heartbeat. A gesture of that sort is appreciated by the receiver and gives you a good feeling for the moment.

This is not to be confused or considered the same as "Put Change Away", but more for trying to get hold of a shopping cart when you need one. They only take a quarter, toonie or a loonie. My only question is "Why do I always get the one with the wobbly wheels?"

# Quotes and Expressions

I enjoy collecting catchy quotations, and even though most are only a line or two, they are full of meaning—as well as cynicism, insults and humour. Here are a few that come to mind:

*Insults/Sarcasm*

- Your gene pool could use a little chlorine.
- Nice perfume. Must you marinate in it?
- If ignorance is bliss, you must be the happiest person alive.

*Golf*

- Who's your caddy?
- One thing about golf is you don't know why you play bad and why you play good.
- 80 percent of golfers cheat. The other 20 percent lie.
- Have you ever noticed what golf spelled backwards is?
- If I hit it right it's a slice, if I hit it left it's a hook, if I hit it straight it's a miracle!

*Words of wisdom*

- I want freedom for the full expression of my personality. (Gandhi)
- Music is the literature of the heart; it commences where speech ends. (Alphonse de Lamartine)
- If you have the words there's always a chance that you'll find the way. (Seamus Heaney)
- There is only one of you in all time, this expression is unique. And if you block it, it will never exist through any other medium and it will be lost. (Martha Graham)
- Everybody is talented because everybody who is human has something to express. (Brenda Leland)

I just pulled these expressions from the Internet, and it took me but 10 minutes to write them down. If you are like myself and really don't enjoy reading much (I get bored too easily), just take a gander through the thousands of these informative quotes and expressions online. They are so powerful, full of passion and full of meaning that can enrich you every day. I know they do for me, and I always find the time to read a few on a daily basis. If nothing else, they should put a smile on your face whether through learning something new or laughing over someone's humour or sarcasm.

# R

Rather Deal With Women
Read Obituary and Birth Columns
Rear in First
Reflect on the Day
Respect Others

# Rather Deal With Women

When it comes to getting things done right the first time and almost to perfection, I have come to the conclusion that women are much better at it than men. Women are going to do their utmost with your best interest in mind, as if they are doing it for themselves, whereas men (sorry) do it for brownie points, bragging rights or their own personal financial gain. That is why I will go out of my way to let a woman handle my affairs, because no matter how miniscule or how big the task, I know I will get the best possible result.

I am proud to say that a woman handles the following important affairs for me:

- financial investments
- banking (there is one exception, and that is Zoran, who handles my personal banking)
- therapist (at one time)
- lawyer
- health (especially nurses)
- auto-repair customer service
- book publishing
- travel planning

Women are more honest, trustworthy, professional and dependable when it comes to helping an individual in any matter. I will be the first in line to combat any argument that says otherwise. I will add one more proof to that, as I ask the question: "Who really is the boss in your house?" I can guarantee that 9 out of 10 men will say the woman.

# Read Obituary and Birth Columns

Take some time from your busy schedule, pick up a newspaper and take a gander at the obituary and birth notices. First off, you must admit that it's quite a relief to not find your name in the obituary column. If you do, then you may be in trouble. My long-time friend Yasu joked with me about this a few years ago. Once you reach a certain age, it does cross your mind, and I am positive that at one time or another a familiar name has been discovered—a friend, co-worker, neighbour, even family member—when glancing through this section.

You can learn quite a bit by reading a little history behind a name. There are some very interesting and different people to be found in the obituaries, each with a unique story. All of the deceased have left a legacy for their families to remember them by. Now they have peace.

I also look at the birth column. It gives me a warm feeling to read about a new life being born into this world. Who knows—he or she could grow up to be our next Prime Minister, Nobel Peace Prize winner, MVP in sports, medal winner at the Olympics or doctor who discovers a cure for cancer. The possibilities are endless.

If nothing else, for quite a few years that child will transform a house into a home full of love, full of joy and full of dreams. That is nothing short of a miracle. It puts a smile on my face every time, and I'm quite sure it will put one on yours. Just for added information, I get a kick out of seeing the weights of some of these babies. Wow!

# Rear in First

I can honestly say that, if a problem arises when trying to leave a parking spot, your best bet is to have backed into the spot in the first place. People are always in a hurry to get somewhere, especially at shopping malls, and without hesitation they pull into the first spot they see without any concern for the possibilities of a problem when they decide to go home.

In older cars especially, batteries do fail, sometimes at no fault of your own other than not doing scheduled maintenance that could identify potential problems down the road (no pun intended). It could be extremely cold weather or lights that were not turned off. It doesn't take much to drain an older battery. If you back into a parking spot, it's much easier to get a boost from someone else to charge the battery or to even hook it up to a tow truck.

Something I'm sure we have all done a few times is put in windshield washer fluid, clear ice from the blades or scrape off ice on the windshield. I have either ruined my pants when trying to squeeze between bumpers or caused expensive dry-cleaning bills. Another problem I have encountered is someone who is parked too close without concern for your difficulty getting out. It is much easier to drive out while going forward rather than back-end first. That is why I try to back in most of the time.

There was one time when I inadvertently drove straight in, and I am so glad I did. I have always said things happen for a reason. Cars on either side of me were parked so close that the doors could not open, and the only way to get in was through the trunk. Thank goodness I was a lot younger and more agile back then.

# Reflect on the Day

At the end of a seemingly never-ending hard day's work, take time when all is quiet to reflect on the events of the day. Take pride in all that you have accomplished, no matter how miniscule it may be. That little accomplishment means one less bit to do tomorrow. Although in most cases, it means you will have one more challenge forthcoming.

Sometimes we have to give ourselves a pat on the back instead of looking for someone to give us one. At least in your mind it's recognized, and that is what it matters most. I did a good job today and can now go home at peace with myself.

By the way, that back-pat does not always have to be about work. It can be helping a co-worker with a task, a selfless act of kindness, opening a door for someone or taking time to give directions to someone who is obviously lost. These acts are all done without accolades, praise or recognition, and that has to make you feel good about yourself.

Unfortunately, there is a downside to this. There might be something you could have done but because of procrastination did not, or you came in 15 minutes late and still left at the normal time, or once again it could be outside of the workplace, like, *Why did I not let that driver in who seemed to be waiting a while for the opportunity to change lanes?*

Once again, these guilt trips may seem small or petty, but they indicate ways we can improve. I think that tomorrow I should go in a little early to get a head start on my project, as it is so quiet in my office early in the morning. It's not a big thing, but once again I can be at peace with myself.

# Respect Others

It will almost always work out as a win-win situation when you acknowledge someone for a good deed, a kind gesture or a task at work, no matter how miniscule it seems to you. You will be pleasantly surprised at the reaction you get from those who may need a little pick-me-up because they're having a bad day, or because another co-worker or a heavy workload has put them in a bad mood. It also makes you feel good knowing you've have made someone smile, even if only for a moment.

Let me give you an example: A middle-aged man and a couple of his friends were laughing out loud at a worker at McDonald's because in their minds, the person was slow and couldn't get their order right. To make this behaviour even more unacceptable, they were using profanity, and not in a low tone of voice. Everyone around could hear, including small children. I'd finally heard enough and asked them in a manner to which they were accustomed to knock off the language. I pointed out that the poor young man was doing the best he could considering how busy he was, and that all of them had to grow up and give people the respect they deserved and expected from others.

The three men (term used loosely) stopped with the language and arrogance, got their order and left quietly with their tails between their legs, as the expression goes. I then thanked the young man and everyone there for their work ethic and told them I appreciated the good service I received there.

The win-win situation in this case was that not only did the people behind the counter thank me for the kind words, but as I was leaving with my coffee and muffin someone ran from behind the counter and handed me the newspaper they had for customers. I was told that he noticed when I came in that I looked to where the papers were placed and there was not one to be found. He took it upon himself to give me one from behind the counter and once again thanked me. Now I was happy and someone else close to me was happy, knowing that the crossword puzzle was coming her way that she used to relax and unwind from her stressful job. So I guess you could say that was my reward.

# S

Safety Pins for Zippers
Self-Appointed Pat on the Back
Set Your Watch a Little Ahead
Show Your Kids the Poor Areas
Smile at a Child
Smile, Not Frown
Stimulate Your Mind
Stop and Smell the Roses
Student Drivers

# Safety Pins for Zippers

Men, how many times have you been ready to go into a meeting, entertain clients at a restaurant or give a speech or pep talk to a group, and just as you are about to take the spotlight, you realize that your zipper is broken? It cannot be just me.

I always get a little nervous before a talk. I am not a president, CEO or political person. Nor am I a motivational speaker by any means. Therefore, when I have the chance to speak in front of people, I always have the tendency and urgency to go tinkle.

More than once I have been in a hurry and, without much concentration, finished my business at the urinal, pulled up my zipper—and either caught it on underwear or T-shirt or just plain broke the zipper. That's what I get for thinking about the topic at hand and peeing at the same time, which leads me to the old adage that "man cannot do more than one thing at a time." Now I would have to walk up to the podium (if there was one) with my notes in front of me, holding them tight with my hands like glue so as not to drop them and expose my mishap.

I have also split my pants in the butt just as I was holding a meeting of baseball coaches (parents) where I was the convener. At least the dads understood, but the mothers who also attended? I'm not so sure. They would shy away from me. That is why I always carry a safety pin in my wallet, and a shoelace, a small container of shoe polish, a paper clip, tape and Band-Aids in my car. You never know when it will happen.

Just in case anyone is wondering, the following are some of the occasions on which I had to give a speech:

- elections for Catholic school-board parent/teacher leaders
- banquets for baseball, which I coached for 19 years
- eulogies at funerals
- speaking as a Boy Scouts scoutmaster

# Self-Appointed Pat on the Back

Patting yourself on the back is justified after a job well done or a disaster avoided. There are times when we don't give ourselves credit for a particular job. It could be something as basic as taking out the garbage on time before the truck arrives—and if all the recycling is done properly, even more reason to feel good about a job that was difficult, but you took the challenge and ran with it.

In my case, I pat myself on the back for making an estimate as accurately as possible, checking to make sure nothing was missed and being able to answer all questions from the powers-that-be before coming up with a price—and all this before the closing date when the price is required. We all need a vote of confidence once in a while, even if it comes from ourselves. We can be our own worst enemy, but it's better to be our own best confidence booster.

The following are a few additional reasons I have for giving myself a pat on the back. There are hundreds of others, but these are some personal ones:

- helping with housework
- going shopping for a few items on the way home from work
- volunteering
- opening a door for someone
- paying bills on time
- setting up electronics
- taking out garbage
- completing a task at the office
- buying a coffee for someone else unexpectedly or for no reason
- Christmas shopping done by the beginning of November
- shovelling snow or cutting grass

# Set Your Watch a Little Ahead

Even if you consider yourself to be regimented when it is important to be on time, there's always a chance that somewhere along the line, for some unknown reason or explanation, you'll be delayed due to factors beyond your control.

I can count on my hands the number of times an alarm clock has actually been beneficial in waking me up on time. Mind you, if I have to get up early to get to the airport or a very early morning meeting, a second alarm is set as a backup just in case. And yet, Murphy's Law applies.

One way to prevent this is to set your clocks and watches at least 5 minutes ahead. In my house, the clocks in the bedroom and bathroom are set 15 minutes ahead, and the clocks in both my cars are set 5 minutes ahead. This is very beneficial because when you are rushing to get going, you probably do not realize the extra time you have until you are well on your way. I guess you could say that tricking yourself provides a psychological advantage. It can also be construed as stress relief. Whatever way you can think of to alleviate stress and frustration from your daily routine, consider it—not only for yourself, but for those around you as well.

# Show Your Kids the Poor Areas

What most of us do when raising a family is work hard (maybe even adding a part-time job), sacrifice a lot and bend over backwards to put a roof over our children's heads, food in their stomachs and clothes on their backs. These are just the essentials that good parents should provide. That is our responsibility. But unfortunately, it doesn't stop there.

Now there are activities children are put in—such as skating, swimming, piano, dancing, sports, school trips and university. Registration is only the beginning of the expenses. You need skates for skating; new swimsuit and goggles for swimming; instrument, stand and books for music lessons; ballet shoes and outfit for dancing; equipment of all sorts for sports. You get the picture. These are just a few of the things that children expect, and in most cases get. We must not forget that parents are also taxi drivers to most of these costly activities—and don't even get me started with kids and cellphones and iPads. They are not necessary.

When two of my children, namely Jason and Nicholas, asked why I couldn't buy them hundred-dollar running shoes and a new game console like their friends had, I tolerated it and just shook it off. There was one time, though, when one of them, I can't remember which, started laying on a guilt trip and asking "Are we poor?" It had been a long day at the office, so it did not take much to push me over the edge. Without hesitation or any concern for what time it was, I picked up my keys. Looking at Jason (who was 11 at the time) and Nicholas (who was 8), I told them sternly to get in the car.

No questions were asked as I drove from Etobicoke to visit a food bank and a hostel on Shuter Street in downtown Toronto. We watched children and adults begging for money and homeless people sleeping over vents with nothing more than a newspaper or a cardboard box ripped apart as a blanket. I saw in both boys' eyes that they had seen enough and been scared enough. No words were spoken from the time we left our house around six in the evening until we returned around ten at night. There was no need to speak. What they saw spoke plenty.

After that, there was no more *I want*, *why not*, begging or guilt trips. It was a true example of "Welcome to the real world and be thankful for what you have, not bitter about what you don't have."

All children should understand and appreciate what their parents do to provide for them. The sacrifice is huge but rewards are plenty when a child shows appreciation. All it takes is a hug or those magic words "I love you." As parents, that's all we ask for. To me, that's my reward.

That is why, to this day, I try to volunteer, although getting lazy lately. Sometimes when I feel depressed for whatever reason, I need a reminder of my blessings. There is nothing more rewarding or fulfilling than helping the less fortunate and hearing someone say thank you. I believe this should be required in schools to encourage our children to see the other side. Then, and only then, will they truly appreciate what their parents do for them. That's when they will realize that their lifestyle is a privilege, not a necessity.

# Smile at a Child

Always smile or wave when you see a child. Most children like a little attention, and when they see a smile or a wave pointed at them, their tendency is to smile back or wave with four fingers and one thumb all out of sync. But the intention is there to return your greeting.

High fives are a bonus. The enthusiasm some kids put into the greeting is remarkable, although the coordination is not always there when the hands come together, especially if the two of you are strangers. This brings me to a little warning: do not attempt to get too close, as you don't want to look creepy. Parents are very protective of their children, as they should be. Play it by ear. Sometimes you may get a puzzled look or a timid look. That's a sign that it's time to move on.

Children are so innocent and naive, but a simple smile or wave does wonders, not only to put a smile on a little one's face but also to make you feel a little younger at heart. That is what adults need every once in a while—just a reminder that a friendly gesture makes everyone's day a little better. It's no fun being miserable, and believe it or not, a child can change that in a moment without even trying.

# Smile, Not Frown

Everyone knows that it takes less effort and fewer muscles to smile than it does to frown. Smiling is a positive expression, as it can be contagious to anyone nearby. I have a tendency to smile a little more when I see someone else enjoying a smile.

On the other hand, I am sure that others think along the same lines as I do: if someone is frowning out of anger, confusion and depression, there is a sudden urge to remove oneself from that environment. Who wants to be dragged into a state of whatever the frown is for?

I know there is another meaning for KISS, but it can be used in this case to mean *Keep It Simple: Smile*. This world would be a better place if there were a lot more smiles and a lot fewer frowns.

# Stimulate Your Mind

It would seem that working 8 to 10 hours a day, five days a week (sometimes six days lately), the brain would have had enough stimulation by week's end—not to mention the additional daily routine of driving 40 minutes to an hour to get to the workplace and then return after a long gruelling day back home. That could be cause for a meltdown for some eventually, but hey, that's the nature of the business. If you don't like it, find another place to get burned out.

But back to the reasons to keep your mind busy. The mind has a tendency to get lazy, and after a while it will go into a sleep mode (just like your computer). Just like your computer, your mind may need to be rebooted from time to time, and it also will have to be updated periodically. That is why doing a crossword puzzle from a daily newspaper, playing a video game (don't get too addicted though by playing too long) and doing brain challenges like math problem-solving and memory challenges is a good idea. Playing solitaire with a deck of cards or Yahtzee with real dice, pencil and paper are a few low-tech examples of how to keep your mind active. I also try to see how close I can get to my bill when I go shopping, mentally adding up the items as they are put in the cart. At the cash register, I try to figure out the tax and see how close I can come to the actual amount.

# Stop and Smell the Roses

This little saying may sound like a cliché and old as heck, but it still has meaning, and it also sends us a strong message that life is short. I have come to realize that life is also a privilege that can be taken from you without warning and at a moment's notice.

How many times have you turned on the TV news, read a newspaper story or I guess these days saw somewhere on the Web that someone was killed today and that their birthday, wedding anniversary, birth of a child, graduation or whatever was only a few days away. We all have busy lives, and I am not going to say that my life has been harder than others, because it hasn't. Still, I need a reminder every once in a while to stop and take a moment to reflect on life in a positive way.

It doesn't matter what you do—think of a loved one, make a phone call to talk to someone close to you, watch a child play and laugh, buy and enjoy an ice cream cone, observe birds in flight—just take a break from what bothers you or from an overload of work and reflect on life, because whether you are alive or not, these little priorities (I call them priorities because they have helped me get through some tough moments) will still be there. Enjoy the little things in life. Somebody should, and it may as well be you. I have added a little to the familiar saying: "Stop and smell the roses, because the day will come, sooner than you think, when you will be the one pushing up daises."

# Student Drivers

Getting a driver's licence these days is like getting a doctor's degree. Back when I got my licence, it was a pretty simple procedure: buy or borrow a driver's manual, read it, memorize a few signs, go to your local MTO office (no appointment necessary), sit down and answer multiple-choice questions (common sense for the most part), hand in your test, wait for a few moments to receive your 365 (temporary permit), walk to another area, show the clerk your 365 and set up a road test. All of this was done within one hour. The actual road test, which came about two weeks later, lasted 10 minutes. It consisted of driving a car through city streets around the MTO office; as long as you did not hit a pole or a pedestrian, did not have more than two horns blasted in your direction and could parallel park your car, you passed and received a full licence with no restrictions or conditions.

Now it's a whole new ball game. I think it goes something like the following:

- Buy and read the manual.
- Pass the eye and written tests for a GI licence with conditions and restrictions, which you keep for 12 months, or 8 months with an approved driver-education course.
- Take the GI road test, which provides you with a G2 licence, also with conditions and restrictions, which you once again keep for 12 months.
- Take the G2 road test, which provides you with a full licence.

I believe this process is known as *graduated licensing*. That is why when driving close to student drivers, as an experienced driver, you should be patient so as not to upset or scare them. Show them courtesy and respect by following the rules and laws that are to be obeyed by all drivers. We are to set an example to our young people, and demonstrating good driving skills and courtesy to other drivers is a way to do that. Don't forget that most of us have gone through this stage.

One added point I would like to make is that maybe a law should be passed forcing seasoned drivers or those with numerous infractions to go back and either redo their driving test or take some sort of mandatory training to be reminded of the rules of the road. It seems that a lot of us have either forgotten or just don't care anymore. It's not always the new drivers who cause trouble, so let's stop knocking them all the time. Respect all drivers on the road. Let's all remember that "driving is a privilege, not a right."

# T

Take Time for Canvassers
Take Time to Reflect
Tip a Little
Treat Yourself

# Take Time for Canvassers

It may seem like a waste of time to talk with a canvasser, but consider the other person and put yourself in his or her situation. Most canvassers do this kind of work, whether by phone or door to door, knowing full well that they are probably going to hear a "not interested," a "bad timing, trying to eat dinner" or a few not so nice words followed by a dial tone or a door being slammed in their face. They may not even get a chance to say what they're selling. Such abuse is very discouraging and disheartening, as this is their job; in most cases, no money is paid to them for their effort until they make a sale.

It's a similar scenario to those who give up their time to volunteer with good intentions as fundraisers. As a person with respect for all jobs, it's important to me in these cases to allow callers a few minutes to give their sales pitch and then courteously reply with an explanation as to why I am not interested in what they are selling—and maybe even thank them for their presentation and wish them good luck in the future.

Realistically, I know that they will be disappointed by another rejection, but at least I have not belittled another human being who is trying to make a buck. I have commented to some on how well their presentation went, how enjoyable and clear their voice is and how well dressed they are, along with the captivating smile they have. At least they have the solace of knowing that not everyone hates them. We all deserve respect. Try to remember that you don't get respect unless you give it.

# Take Time to Reflect

Every day, I take a little time from my hectic routine to think of something that has made me happy in the past, or something that will be making me happy in the near future. Those few minutes daily are similar to taking a yoga class. Thinking of nice things (in Adam Sandler's movie *Happy Gilmore*, he mentions a "happy place") is like meditating. It can be so peaceful and relaxing and rewarding, all without leaving your present location or wearing those silly tights worn in yoga class. All I do is close my office door, close my eyes and think of a happy place.

Recently, we booked a trip for July, approximately six months from now. It's easy to forget today's stress, anger, anxiety and sadness, and concentrate on the preparation ahead all the way to the experience itself. I also use my children and grandchildren as visuals in my mind to help me "think happy" at times. It doesn't take much, but a simple break in the midst of an awkward or difficult task at hand can actually help you through it a lot easier and faster than you think.

Something to ponder or think about, right?

# Tip a Little

Although there is an unwritten rule that one must tip at least 15 percent at a restaurant, it should not be forced down your throat as an automatic procedure at every place you visit where service is provided—especially if that service is not up to your expectations. Unfortunately, there seems to be that "taken for granted" attitude in the more expensive places.

Many years ago, when the entire in-law family went out for New Year's dinner, there must have been some nasty phrases said after I left this well-known restaurant. My memory does not serve me well at this time, so I can't give a name, but the night went as follows: We had to wait to be seated, even after a reservation was made and confirmed before we all got there. The food was not bad, but it was not the best of quality or quantity. The service was not the best, as it should have been, and the bill had items that were not ordered by anyone.

When I paid the bill, I put down a tip that was not to the server's liking, I guess, as I heard him mutter to the other server about how cheap I was. I believe he said it loud enough for me to hear as an attempt to give me a guilt trip so I would change the amount.

That was a mistake. I took the bill, looked at the waiter, and said something like, "Sorry, I should not have put that amount in." He gave me a sheepish smile. I then changed it to a big zero and said, "That's what you truly deserve." I walked out after paying at the front with not an ounce of guilt. I will not buy into anything that is shoved down my throat. Like I said, I'm sure nasty phrases were said after I left. You get what you pay for—but as well, you get paid for what you do. So do it right!

To be perfectly honest, I would much rather leave a tip for someone who works in a coffee shop or a relatively small or unknown family restaurant, as they truly are working for peanuts. Although they don't expect a huge tip, you know that it will be greatly appreciated. The smile you get and the thanks make it all worthwhile. The service will be the same if not better the more times you frequent that establishment.

# Treat Yourself

This is a very important topic, especially since most of us work extremely hard to provide for our family. That means paying all sorts of bills. Add the stress of work that we have to endure in order to pay those bills that help provide for our family—without hearing thank you most of the time—and the time we spend in the car, bus, train, subway or streetcar to get to work. On top of that, add the cost of gas, maintenance and insurance for the car, or the never-ending rise in the cost of fares just to take the transit to work. Not to mention the taxes we pay. It goes on and on and on. When was the last time you stopped and gave yourself a treat?

It could be as simple as taking time away from the hustle and bustle of everyday nonsense and enjoying anything from a coffee and a muffin (my favourites) in a cafe to a nice cold beer and wings (sound good to me, but I don't drink) outdoors on a patio to something as expensive as a night out on the town or buying a new video system, which I have done. The treat does not have to be elaborate, but if you have the funds, by all means go for it. Do what makes you feel better. Heck, I even enjoy sitting in the park on a bench with a newspaper or book basking in the sunshine and watching the people around me.

You don't have to do anything very elaborate, but if you don't do something for yourself, no one else will!

# U

Underestimate No One
Under the Weather

# Underestimate No One

After many years of fighting to get to where I am today, it came to me that none of us has an automatic entitlement to the top of the totem pole. Whether in sports or business or any walk of life, no one should have the audacity to believe that there will not be a challenge from someone else to dethrone them. Take sports, for example. There are too many stories regarding underdogs versus the big guys to remember. How many times has the one who was supposed to lose ended up winning the big game?

The same ideology applies to the business world. Once people are comfortable in a high position, there can be a tendency to slack off and get a little too complacent. If you think that no one is watching and no one has a clue as to what is going on, you are only fooling yourself. Never underestimate the people around you, as they could be smarter than you are giving them credit for. It is an insult to their intelligence. Don't forget, they have been there themselves and gone through what you are going through, so they know how the system works and how the games are played. At my place of employment, trust is a key factor for working, and you have to earn the trust, like most places.

Your work ethic is what got you to where you are today, so don't forget to upgrade or fine-tune that once in a while. Getting lazy and taking shortcuts is a sign of disinterest and shows the boss that you are not up for the same challenges you once were. Employers notice these traits in their employees. I know they do at my office, and that's why I strive to improve, even at my age. That's the way I was brought up—not only for my job but to prove to myself that I can maintain the same enthusiasm and interest I had while growing up and starting in the business.

I was always classified as the underdog. I felt like David versus Goliath at times, and I was always underestimated, but I always managed to beat the odds when it counted. My company notices things like that, and that is why it's a company that is getting bigger and better every day.

# Under the Weather

Why is it that when we as humans—and especially the male gender—get sick, get a headache or get disappointed, it is our nature to feel sorry for ourselves or look for sympathy from those close to us? Being "under the weather," as the expression goes, may work for a while, but your significant other can only take so much of you pushing the envelope. Instead of causing friction around the house, why not pass the time away by catching up on all the tedious jobs that are staring you in the face—filing paperwork, sorting things out or organizing pictures? If you can, why not do a little home repair by tightening up a loose faucet or hanging a picture, which you promised to do quite a while ago? Why not help around the house by doing chores? That's always good for a few brownie points.

Doing these little odd jobs should make you feel better—if not physically, then certainly mentally, and as we all know sickness can be a state of mind. Getting things off your to-do list is important, because in most households, it's never-ending.

# V

Valentine's Day—Why?

# Valentine's Day—Why?

I honestly have a problem with this day of romance. Do we (men in particular) actually need a reminder to say or show how much we are in love with someone? To me it is just a marketing ploy, giving us such a guilt trip that we buy things because we have so much shame or guilt. According to a *National Geographic* study, an average of $14.7 million was spent on Valentine's Day in 2009. The cost is staggering!

I believe our loved ones should be reminded every day about how much they are loved, appreciated and cared for. You don't need goofy cards, unhealthful chocolates and expensive flowers to show how much you care. That's only one day out of the year. What about the other 364 days? To me, if you're only focusing on this one day a year, you're taking your partner for granted.

To be honest, I have made several assumptions, bad judgments and errors in my marriage. After 24 years, it ended. Although it takes two to tango, as the expression goes, I never once wondered and expressed anger, ridicule or blame towards the other person in the relationship. I concentrated on my own self.

To this day, I try to express my gratitude (I do need reminders at times) by thanking my significant other every day—with a thank you for a well-cooked meal, a lunch prepared the night before, help shovelling snow, a hot coffee on a cold morning, a hug or smile for no reason, sharing secrets, cuddling and sitting on the couch together.

In my case, I cannot cook for beans; I even managed to burn a pot when boiling water. So every once in a while, we go to our favourite place for a meal. I bring home flowers from time to time without any reason or without an apology or motive. It is just a simple way of saying thank you, and hopefully the gesture is appreciated.

I remember last February, when I was in Verona's flower store in Woodbridge, the line on Valentine's Day in the afternoon was out the door. It is not a huge store, but there had to be at least a dozen men waiting to pick up flowers for their better half. To me, they were there not out of love or compassion but out of guilt. If they forgot, they would be in the doghouse—hence the trip to the flower shop. Pitiful in my eyes.

# W

Wallet in Your Front Pocket
Watch Children Play
Water From the Sky
Weather and Conversation
Willing to Help
Work Before Play
Worry About Snow
Write Poetry

# Wallet in Your Front Pocket

When I was 12, while visiting the CNE, I had my wallet picked from my pants pocket. I didn't find out until I went to pay for some french fries and a soft drink that it was no longer with me. The loss of all my money (about twenty dollars) and a few TTC tickets made for both embarrassment at the moment and the start of an even bigger dilemma. How would I get home? I had become separated from a friend earlier in the day, so borrowing a TTC ticket was not an option. There were no cellphones back then, and I had no backup plan. Being extremely shy and reserved back then, after a couple of rejections from people I had asked for a ticket, I saw walking as my only alternative. Four hours later and way past curfew, exhaustion set in, so much that even when being grounded for missing curfew I did not have the strength to argue my case.

Ever since that time, my wallet has always been in my front pocket when visiting crowded places like a flea market or a busy mall at Christmas. Even when I'm travelling with all of my prized possessions—such as a camera, passport, credit card, driver's licence—they will be either in my front pocket, in a waist pouch or directly in front of me on some sort of contraption around my neck. If any attempt to steal that happens, my head goes with it. Also, whenever I'm travelling, I wear pants with buttons, snaps or zippers on the front pockets for a little added protection.

Even if it is only psychological, it's worth it. The last thing you need when travelling is a lost or stolen document. It's not only embarrassing, but it can be hard to correct and can make for complications and delays trying to get home.

# Watch Children Play

As parents we are supposed to be role models for our children. We are expected to be teachers, mentors, providers and protectors. Recently I watched a video that was made by an Australian organization known as Napcan, which helps prevent child abuse. The video shows explicit scenes of parents texting/talking while crossing the street, parents smoking, parents butting out their cigarettes, parents tossing empty pop cans on the street, parents yelling profanities with middle finger at other drivers, parents verbally or physically abusing their partner and parents physically abusing and destroying a public phone. All of these actions were witnessed by their children, and wouldn't you know it, they were doing the same things as the video. Experts say, "Children see, children do."

We may not realize it but children are smarter than we give them credit for. They pick up everything they see, and in their minds, if Mom and Dad do it, it must be all right. They look up to us for everything they do.

We must do a better job of showing our children right and wrong. If you want to get a little bit of insight on how we can learn from children, all you have to do is watch them play—in the park, in the schoolyard, in a sport, in front of a TV, at a party or in their bedroom.

We can learn so much just by observing! Children do not care what colour their playmate is. Children do not care if their playmate has a physical or mental challenge. Children do not care who wins or loses a game. Children do not care what they get for presents at parties. Children do not care what game they play. Children do not care what age or gender their playmate is.

Children are so innocent among their own—without prejudice, racism, hatred, anger, destruction, words that hurt or actions of violence against one another. I truly believe that children act out because of what they see and hear from within their home. The questions I would put forward to parents would be the following:

- Could your home environment be poisonous and be a contributing factor to your child's misbehaviour?
- Could anything you say to your children be followed up with, "Maybe you should look in the mirror?"

It is a privilege to be around children. They are beautiful, talented, wonderful, happy, loving, innocent, articulate, full of energy, intelligent, caring little men and women. Although I have had and still am having fun with my four children (Jason, Nicholas, Andrew and Jennifer), I have put away enough good memories and proud moments to keep my storybook full for a long, long time.

# Water From the Sky

Try a little experiment with your lawn and tell me if you agree or disagree. Whether you notice it right away or not, you will probably come to the same conclusion as I have, and that is that water that falls from the sky—whether a gentle, steady shower or an all-out blusterous thunderstorm—seems to bring out the best in your lawn a day later. A day of steady, compassionate, time-consuming watering of your grass by hand does not give the same result.

The grass is greener, thicker and longer (weeds too, unfortunately) when water from the heavens falls. The same can be said for gardens, floral or vegetable—they become more colourful, more full, more abundant, more everything. It's Mother Nature's way of telling us that you can save some time and effort by letting her take care of the earth so you can spend a little more time with other important things in life. These would be family and friends— or in my case family, friends and a little golf. I keep telling myself this when I leave early Saturday or Sunday to play a round; it helps get rid of the guilt.

# Weather and Conversation

As silly as this may sound, I personally believe that there is a strong similarity between weather and peoples' personalities. Have you ever noticed how cheerful, bubbly and energetic we are on a beautiful, warm, sunny day, but when the weather is not so favourable, we become miserable, lazy and lethargic? Why is that? Every day should be embraced, experienced and enjoyed to the fullest. Just because it doesn't meet our standards doesn't mean we can't enjoy it.

Another point to ponder would be, "Maybe it's a sign." Have you ever noticed that when two total strangers from what seem to be opposite ends of the universe begin a conversation, it usually starts with an opening line regarding the weather? A response follows, and the next thing you know, communication is flowing between two people who would not normally exchange words. It's simply amazing.

There has always been one puzzling question when I listen to a weather forecast, and that is, why do they say, for example, 50 percent chance of rain, 50 percent chance of sun? Is that how they cover their rear end for protection, or are they playing the odds for a bet at Vegas? Just wondering.

# Willing to Help

It will go a long way in a relationship—whether with a friend, a co-worker or a neighbour—if you provide help even when it's not asked for. It may not mean much to you at the time, but it will more than likely be remembered by the one receiving your kindness or effort. At the time you do help, it will just seem like the thing to do, but you will be surprised how fast that person will jump in to help you down the road, even without being asked—probably when you least expect it, and probably with a smile. As I always say, "It's better to give than receive."

# Work Before Play

This topic should be understood and appreciated at an early age. Parents should teach the concept that work, scheduled or not, should be done before play—and done properly the first time. As an example: There are times when I don't feel like cutting the grass, knowing that I am going out later or tomorrow to enjoy a round of golf with friends. Part of me says I will do it when I return from golf. It rarely gets done, however, as I feel tired after walking around for four or four and a half hours. If my math serves me right, walking five to five and a half kilometres as the crow flies is the norm, but in my case, it's more like six to six and a half, as rarely do I hit the ball straight. Walking in the sun chasing and looking for a little white ball to hit into a four-inch cup in the fewest shots possible tires you out, and if the round is a bad one, you definitely won't feel like doing any chores when you get home. Trust me, I've been in that situation.

When those times arise, knowing that work comes first and not being in the mood to get into it, I put my golf bag on the driveway as an incentive to remind me what's next after my chore is done. It works most of the time.

Believe it or not, you will do a better job before rather than later, and that is also a good thing. If a job is not done right, you will know about it, and there will be consequences. If you are an employee, your boss will let you know; if you are a child, your parents will let you know; and if you are a husband, your wife will let you know, again and again and again. So my suggestion is, do the required or requested work before play, as it will make everybody involved happy, especially yourself.

# Worry About Snow

Why is it that when a storm is predicted or snow begins to fall, we humans seem to get all anxious and stressed out about it? There is no scientific proof that worrying about a storm will make it go away.

Therefore, save yourself any anxiety and do what most children do: embrace it. Go outside and enjoy it. Feel the fresh air. Touch the snowflakes, and make the best out of the situation. I know it's hard to do when you have to drive in the stuff to get to work, but if you can take a snow day, sit back and enjoy frolicking around in one of nature's many beautiful settings. Children do, and when you're done playing, nothing beats warming up inside with a cup of hot chocolate with a marshmallow floating on top. It's even more special when you share it with someone.

I have always said that we as adults should not only teach our children by setting good examples for them but also learn from our children and enjoy every day, regardless of the situation. Instead of worrying what snow has done to you, go out and see what you can do to the snow. I like building a snowman, cross-country skiing, skating and shovelling for a little exercise and fresh air. Children embrace snow, so why not do the same as adults?

# Write Poetry

Before I get into this topic, an explanation is necessary. You see, a lot of professionals deal with a lot of stress. At times, stress can really get to you or be overwhelming, unless you can eliminate it before you go crazy.

Some people go shopping, some people go to the golf course to smack a few balls (I do that but it still doesn't help my game), some people drink, some people smoke and some people scream to help them cope with their day-to-day stress. Being part Scots, I rule shopping out, as it means spending money. Hitting a few golf balls does not work, as it tends to make aches in my back flare up. My game still has not improved. I have never tried smoking and do not intend to start now.

Drinking to me is a waste of time other than to celebrate a birthday, a toast at a wedding, a New Year's celebration or maybe a BBQ with friends. I can be silly without being drunk. Besides, drinking can be expensive in a public place. There goes the Scots in me again.

There have been personal issues with screaming as well as anger that I am not too proud of, but I have graduated from that childish act. So I write lines of things that make me relax or make me smile. You would be surprised what you can come up with, and just for your information, when writing poetry, the words don't always have to rhyme.

Guys, here is a little secret if you don't know it already. Ladies love to have someone close to them put down a few words of love, caring and compassion with them in mind. Can you imagine the surprise when she sees these handwritten words that she thought you could not even spell, let alone know what they mean? You might even get lucky. And even if you don't succeed with what you tried to put down in words, she will understand and commend you on the effort.

Unfortunately, I tend to go to the humorous way of expression and will leave you with one of my favourites. I believe it's known as a limerick. My age shows here, as you would have to know a half-hour TV show from the late 1940s to late 1950s called *The Lone Ranger*. It was about a cowboy with a mask and his Indian (native) friend Tonto, doing good deeds and catching bad guys. You also would have watched it on a black-and-white television. The limerick goes as follows:

There once was a cowboy from Toronto,
Who had an Indian friend named Tonto,
Whom when found out what Kemo Sabe meant,
All his money was spent,
To buy a new gun to kill Tonto and pronto.

## X-Rays Aren't Always Enough

# X-Rays Aren't Always Enough

There was a time in my life when I was young (yes, I was young once), carefree and full of vim and vigour, as they say—when I didn't know the meaning of the words *pain* and *consequences*. Young people think they are invincible. Yet there were so many hospital visits due to silly acts of my own doing (plus some imposed upon me by those with no remorse or respect for the rules of the game) that I honestly cannot remember them all.

Consider the following scenario when an old timer attempted to play a little shinny with a group of guys a few years back. I will sum up what happened in a sentence: while playing in net, he wandered behind the net, took a cross check to the back of the head that forced the front of his head (wearing a mask, thank goodness) against the glass of the back boards and then fell straight down onto the ice with the back of his head again. The result, not surprisingly, was a concussion. Over the next three weeks, while having his little brain looked at, he was told that something else was not right. Follow-up tests showed there was another issue that has since been taken care of.

If not for the follow-up tests after the X-rays—such as MRIs, scans and ultrasounds—the problem would not have been found or diagnosed. Other than headaches, which come and go as they please and which he has learned to live with, he has no other issues regarding the experience.

What I am trying to emphasize is, when you go to a hospital for a problem and an X-ray is negative, don't take the doctor's word that all is well. You know your body better than anyone. If you continue to feel something is not right, or different symptoms and feelings arise, follow up with a physician and insist on more tests or a look in a different direction as to what the problem could possibly be. No offence to doctors, as they do a wonderful job and are underappreciated at times, but they are not God, and sometimes their ego can get in the way. There are a few who don't like to hear words such as, "Can you look in this direction? or "I don't agree with you" or "Maybe you are wrong." I wish these doctors would drop the ego and realize they are human, and humans can make mistakes.

I proved them wrong when I took a different approach towards my dilemma at the time. Words were exchanged, but I stuck to my guns as to how the problem was to be tackled, and hopefully, at the time, I made the right decision. My way prevailed. That's all I have to say. Just to add a little comment to what happened: At the time, I was a very angry at the person who nailed me. After all, it was a game of non-contact for a group of men over 40. But I have come to forgive the man, and that was long before the discovery of my dilemma. As the expression goes, "There is a silver lining behind every cloud." Or, my favourite: "Things happen for a reason."

# Y

Youth and Obesity

# Youth and Obesity

This category leaves me not only disturbed but also frustrated and angry—at the young people who are obviously overweight but even more so at the parents for allowing their children to get to that point. Obesity is not a genetic thing; it's a choice thing. If you allow your children to indulge in an unhealthy diet, constantly eat fast foods, drink pop and go crazy at buffets, then the blame should be partly on your shoulders. Parents are supposed to set an example, and what better or more important way to do that than to teach kids healthy eating habits and what can happen later in life if you don't have them.

Heart attack, diabetes and depression are only a few risks that come to mind. There are plenty more out there. I frequent these fast-food places to grab a coffee and a muffin; since I do not drink or smoke, I feel that I am allowed these little treats once in a while. I see families there, and at times I am overwhelmed by the amount of food purchased by the parents for themselves and their children. What makes these purchases mind-boggling is that the majority of the parents are overweight, and their kids are heading in the same direction. It's just too bad that not only are the parents at risk for health problems related to being overweight but now they are setting their kids off on the same route.

Another reason parents should be more to blame is that they allow their kids to sit and vegetate while watching television, playing video games and socializing on the computer, whereas they should be encouraging the youngsters to go outdoors and play with friends or participate in organized sports to get the exercise they need. All of my kids were active in activities outside of the home. Whether it was baseball, hockey, soccer, swimming, dancing or running, they all willingly participated—and it shows today. When I was young, there were no computers, no cellphones and no video games, so there was no choice but to play outdoors.

And parents, please stop driving your children everywhere, like dropping them off at school, dropping them off two blocks from home at a school-bus pickup point or taking them to the mall. Let them walk. That's why God gave them two feet.

# Z

## Zs Are Good for You

# Zs Are Good for You

There used to be a time when being caught dozing off—whether at the airport, at your office desk, on a park bench, in a chair in a waiting room or in a car—was looked upon as a lazy, silly and funny way of presenting yourself to others. Now it's known as power-napping. When I was a backup goaltender in hockey, I used to have naps on the bench, at least until my coach would tap me on the back of my mask and say, "Wake up, your snoring is distracting the team."

I believe that napping from time to time has been analysed and found to be good for you. It energizes your brain and helps you to be more alert and more productive at the same time. That's if you do it right. Dozing off is not wise or acceptable while driving, only while in the passenger seat. The following method is the best way I have found to nap:

- Find a good place to nap. At work, it could be a place provided by your employer. On the road, pull over, turn the car off, put on the emergency brake and turn off your mobile phone and other distractions. Maybe put on headphones and listen to music.
- Have caffeine right before you nap. It takes time for caffeine to travel through your system (about forty-five minutes). When you wake up after a 20-minute nap, it will help your performance.
- When you're close to finishing your coffee or tea, set an alarm to go off in 15 minutes.
- Outside your office door, which should be closed at this point, post a sign that says you are power-napping and can be contacted at a certain time.
- Get up as soon as the alarm goes off. Sleeping more than 20 minutes is counterproductive. Sleeping more than 30 minutes can lead to sleep inertia, which makes you sluggish and more tired.

I must share this story with you. My friend Kwan used to take power naps. He did this long before it was discovered to be a good thing. We all knew he was more intelligent than others. We worked together at a construction company in which Kwan was a draftsperson, and my office desk was at the other end of the room, approximately 20 to 25 feet away from his drawing board. I must note, it was an open-concept office. No walls between us.

Once or twice a day, you would stop hearing his machine go back and forth while he was working on a drawing, and then you would hear him snoring. If it got really intense, you would hear a bang as his head hit the board, which would wake him up in most instances. We would not see him, as the back of his board blocked our view of him. But let me tell you, after every power nap, Kwan would be more focused in his work and would go like a "bat out of hell," as the expression goes.

# 3

# THOUGHTS TO PONDER (ON THE LIGHTER SIDE)

# A

Abbreviations: Make Up Phrases
Altered Bones Can Tell Weather

# Abbreviations: Make Up Phrases

This is a little game that I amuse myself with at times when there is a need to take a break from a stressful project or to help pass a little time when stuck in traffic. Instead of getting stressed or frustrated, try playing with letters (normally I use ones from licence plates) and coming up with your own sayings. This is just a meaningless little exercise when trying to pass a few minutes without going crazy. For example, the following are just a few of my favourites, and although they are considered acronyms that I have used from time to time with the first three being original they are either funny or have meaning nonetheless.

- **TGIF** (not "Thank God It's Friday"): I've mentioned my version of this somewhere else in the book but it also could be put on top of my shoes which means "Toes Go In First"
- **KOBSWNB**: No names mentioned, but this applies to a particular person who loves letters after his name but does not have the courage to discipline certain employees who do not follow a certain work protocol: King Of BullS... With No Balls
- **PITA**: Pain In The Ass
- **CLASS**: Come Late And Start Sleeping
- **USCWNP**: Up S... Creek With No Paddle
- **TEAM**: Together Everyone Achieves More
- **MATH**: Mental Abuse To Humans
- **GREAT**: Get Really Excited About Today (personal favourite)
- **WATER**: Wonderful And Totally Energizing Refreshment
- **LOLz**: Laugh Out Loud (sarcastically)
- **NNWW**: Nudge Nudge Wink Wink
- **FBSOAL**: Few Bricks Short Of A Load
- **ERBNOBTH**: Engine Running But No One Behind The Wheel
- **FIGJAM**: F... I'm Good Just Ask Me
- **ATM:** Automatic Teller - Mom

# Altered Bones Can Tell the Weather

I used to think that this was just an old foolish tale, but after numerous knee issues (including cartilage problems) and one meniscus problem, let me tell you I have truly become a believer. Those injuries happened a long time ago, so from my late teens to my mid-twenties, if memory serves me right, approximately 10 to 12 hours before it rains my knee will start to nag me in a way that's hard to explain. It's kind of like an annoying itch—or like the slight tingling feeling when your arm wakes up, as the saying goes, after it seems lifeless for a bit because it's been in an awkward position. It's not painful at all, but it's very noticeable when the weather is going to change in the near future.

It becomes beneficial when planning to play golf or any outdoor activity. In fact, my leg has become more reliable and accurate than many a forecast from the radio or TV. If I could only find a way for it to give me a temperature reading, I might just make some extra money predicting the weather. And I am not even a meteorologist. Sometimes I think that they throw darts at a dartboard and where it lands, that's the prediction.

# B

Before You Sit on the Toilet
Belly Button Lint
Birds and Clean Cars

# Before You Sit on the Toilet

How many times, especially if you are a male, have you gone into the bathroom, closed the door, dropped your pants, dropped your shorts and then sat down to have a few minutes of solitude as you enjoy a nice healthy movement—only to find out that there is no toilet paper (usually when you're at the point of needing it)? It is important to make note of this before you sit down; once your deed is done, it's too late to do the normal wipe and wash routine. Trying to find a replacement roll can be difficult at the best of times.

An example of this from my own experience: After I realized that the holder was empty, I knew there were more rolls in a cabinet directly in front of me. It was only a step away ... or so I thought. I reached out and struggled to open the cabinet door from a sitting position. It was at that point a new problem was discovered. The rolls were near the back of the cabinet. Without hesitation, my left arm reached out and into the cabinet without regard for what could and did happen next. I stretched so far that my rear end slipped off the seat and plopped on the ceramic floor.

It was embarrassing enough trying to explain the thump heard throughout the house, but it was even more evident that this was just the beginning of my trying moment. On my way up, as I grabbed the towel rack to raise myself, wouldn't you know it, off the wall it came—screws, plugs and drywall. Now I not only had to do a major cleaning job on the ceramic floor (remember, I still hadn't wiped myself yet), but I had to repair the wall and reinstall the towel rack. All of that work I can honestly say was a pain in the butt, both physically and mentally.

In short, and this is for the men of the house, please take a piece of advice as you carefully read the following:

1.  Make sure there is toilet paper on the roll, both when you enter and when you leave.
2.  When finished, put the lid down. My dad, come to think of it, had a wooden sign in the bathroom directly over

the toilet at the cottage in Wasaga Beach that read, "If you sprinkle when you tinkle, be a sweetie and wipe the seatee." A few words of wisdom to live by so you don't get a lecture from your better half.

# Belly Button Lint

It does not matter what type of shirt we wear—undershirt, cotton, polyester, short-sleeved, long-sleeved, T-shirt, no shirt—or how often we wash our clothes, the lint, hair and fibres still manage to build up in our belly button. The longer you leave the lint alone, the more there seems to be. It's like some little creature or alien is building a nest in there. Weird!

# Birds and Clean Cars

What gives with birds and clean cars? How many times have you washed your car and then innocently and without thought parked it like everyone else in a public place. You go inside to carry on with your daily routine—ten minutes in a bank, a couple of hours in a mall shopping, an hour or so for an important meeting—only to find upon your return that your vehicle's been dumped on, to put it mildly.

Of all the vehicles in the lot, it seems these feathered friends do a flyover and pick out the cleanest vehicle they can see, and then it's bombs away. If their deposits aren't cleaned off right away, the stuff becomes hard, crusty and very tough on the nose.

So do yourself a favour. When you get a car wash, put the car in a garage or cover it with a tarp because you know they will be looking for you.

# C

Chip Bags
Cricket—What's With the Scoring?
Customs Agents

# Chip Bags

There must be a better way of packaging potato chips. The bags make so much noise that it's virtually impossible to sneak the satisfying snack without sharing it with others. There are times when, watching a game on the television or at a movie, that one would like to be selfish. People drown their sorrows while drinking; why can't I watch my beloved Maple Leafs, Blue Jays and Argonauts and drown my sorrows over their losses, which come quite often, by munching down some chips? After all, I can legally get behind the wheel and drive home afterwards.

Maybe the wives and the mothers of children have something to do with this. Hearing a bag open up automatically brings guilt with the look of a mother glaring down at her child or a wife angrily eyebrowing her husband, as if it's a sin to eat those addictive, crunchy little bits of heaven—especially without sharing. So please, someone invent a noiseless bag for people like me who just want to indulge in one of life's little pleasures without having any guilt or injustice cast over us.

# Cricket—What's With the Scoring?

In cricket, the following scoring takes place:

- number of runs scored
- number of wickets lost
- number of overs bowled

It's a fascinating game to watch, but unlike most sports, the scoring has me totally perplexed as to who the winner might be. In baseball, hockey or football, for example, the one with the highest score wins. You know—one number compared to another. The higher score wins unless you are playing golf, in which case the lower score wins (exceptions to every rule). Track and field is easy. If I cross the finish line before you, I win. But don't get me started on tennis. Where did the scoring 15-30-40-game come from? There is no uniformity or logic to that sequence, but again, the higher number of sets won determines the winner.

I just wish someone would spend some time and explain the scoring system for cricket, so I could appreciate the sport with a little more enthusiasm and understanding.

# Customs Agents

Is it just me, or are the vast majority of customs agents and security people miserable and unhappy with what they're doing? I know they have a job that is extremely important yet thankless, one that most travelers hardly notice except to complain about it. Their professionalism and expertise allow for a safe trip, and for that undertaking I am forever grateful. But I wish they would smile once in a while. It's not going to kill them.

Let me give you one example: A few years back, I was on my way home from a trip abroad. It was extremely crowded and a little chaotic, as you'd expect for a late in the afternoon at the airport. I guess it can be compared to rush hour driving in the city. All of us were being asked to remove our watches, take change from our pockets and take off our shoes. This one agent asked for everyone wearing a belt to remove it.

Without hesitation, I jokingly, with a smile, looked at her and said, "If my belt comes off, my pants will fall down." I thought it was an innocent few words to break the stress for a moment with a bit of humour, but to my surprise her reply was, and I quote, "*Sir, take your f\*\*king belt off, NOW.*" I can think of the following reasons why she would behave this way:

1. Maybe it's the end of a 30-day cycle.
2. Envy of those travelling while she is stuck at work.
3. Always had dreams of being a police officer but did not quite meet all the qualifications.
4. End of a very long shift (been there, done that).
5. Has the mindset of a Sheldon from *The Big Bang Theory* TV show and loves to show off authority and intelligence.

I know that it can be very stressful at times with a lot of silly people delaying the lines by either not being prepared or being totally ignorant of what they are legally expected to do. Come to think of it, I probably would react the same way at times, and more than likely I'd be fired on the first day. They do a terrific job, and I am very thankful for the job they do, but maybe a sense of humour once in a while would make their job a little easier.

# D

Dirt Under the Couch
Drive-Throughs

# Dirt Under Couch

I've been on my own since my early teens, and again from age 47 until now at a ripe old 62, and I still find it to be a mystery as to the amount of dirt that builds up under furniture. I may not be the best candidate to work for Molly Maid, but I do like to live in a relatively clean and tidy home. Yet whether I use a broom, a rag, a Swiffer picker-upper or a central vacuum, there seems to be just as much stuff under a couch as there is on the floor I walk on—sometimes even more. It's like there are really tiny miniscule critters bringing in this dust from somewhere, leaving it, and then going into hiding and waiting until I reach under to get the dust out (probably hurting my back or cutting my hand on something in the process) while laughing among themselves.

# Drive-Throughs

People use the drive-through, I am told, so they can save some time rather than going into the coffee shop. I regularly visit different places with drive-throughs and have done my own survey (something tells me that I should get a life). I have come to the conclusion that I can park my car at the very same time someone drives into the lane designated for drive-through, get out and walk 50 to 100 feet to get inside, order my coffee and donut, have a moment to ask the friendly person behind the counter how he or she is doing, wish that worker a nice day, walk out with my coffee and donut in hand, walk another 50 to 100 feet to get to my car—and look over to at the drive-through line to see the same cars that were there when I entered, still waiting to get their order. So let's be honest: it doesn't save time, you're just too lazy to get out of the car. I know for a fact that a majority of those people need to get out and walk a little bit, not to mention stop polluting the air as they're waiting.

# E

English Sportscaster
Eulogies Can Be Fun
Exams in School ... Why?
Express Lines 1–8

# English Sportscasters

Please do not pass judgment on what I am about to say, sportscasters. Over the year, I have witnessed and listened to dozens of sportscasters on television and radio; some are very good at what they do, while others may know the sports business but really don't come across to the viewer as any more knowledgeable than an audience member.

Over the past little while, I've noticed a few English sportscasters coming onto the scene doing North American sportscasts on television—or should I start saying "telly"? Although they are extremely intelligent—or should I start saying "bloody brilliant"?—it's hard to keep a straight face when hearing someone with an English accent talk about a hockey game, a baseball game, or a football game. To me, the English have been stereotyped into doing cricket matches, rugby matches, soccer games and tennis matches. Heck, I even enjoy their commentary on billiards and dart competitions. It's just a matter of time before I think nothing of it, but for now I will do my utmost to accept them as professionals doing their job. They are great at what they do; it's just the accent I have to get used to.

I also hear that there is "Punjabi Night in Canada" relating to hockey, although that will be hard to get used to. I think it's terrific that all these different cultures are getting into our sports. The diversity Canada stands for is great for everyone—even for me.

# Eulogies Can Be Fun

We tend to be so serious when a loved one or a close friend passes away. Why is that? I know that you are supposed to show your sadness, mourn for the person, pray for the family, make an appearance at the viewing and send flowers out of respect. If the deceased is family, you must bury the person with the love, respect and dignity he or she deserves. Then, after the procession and burial, there is usually a get-together at a local restaurant or someone's home; I prefer the latter, as it is a little less formal and more relaxed. After all is said and done, you must pull yourself together and get back to a normal routine—although I do admit it, it takes time to do that.

That's where eulogies come in. They're a chance to say goodbye in a happy way. Eulogies tend to focus on the good in the person who just passed away. But in reality, no one is perfect. Why not let family and friends in the pew or at the gathering after the service complete the picture of the real person with some of his or her not-so-great attributes? Participants could share that the deceased:

- made bogus claims on income-tax returns to get a refund or pay less tax;
- had extramarital affairs;
- cheated on exams to successfully obtain a university degree;
- stole from a local store;
- fibbed about education in order to get a job or impress someone;
- sabotaged someone at work to get the person fired or at least disciplined;
- hit a car in a parking lot and left without telling anyone; or
- stepped on a neighbour's plants (deliberately).

These are just a few of the many lines you could add to a eulogy. I have been to a few funerals where some of these lines would have applied, knowing the real person—but then I thought to myself that my day will come as well, and I was a little farther from perfect than my predecessors. So leave it alone!

I have done eulogies for my father; my two sisters, Vera and Dorothy; my close friend of about four decades, Kwan; and my nephew Gerry. I had nothing but love and praise and respect for them. So all that was said was from the heart.

I also think that there is an old saying that goes something like, "If you have nothing nice to say, then say nothing at all." Great words to live by.

# Exams in School—Why?

In high school back in the mid- to late 1960s, I began to ponder the relevance of exams, especially since they made up anywhere from 30 to 50 percent of the final mark on my report card.

It made no sense to me then, and it makes no sense to me now—although I am out of touch with how the system works today as to why there is so much emphasis put on exams. It's not like you're going to be tested the same way in the real world. In the real world, there are numerous resources at your fingertips for resolving problems and discovering new and necessary answers to the questions we encounter on a daily basis. There are answers everywhere—from old-fashioned library books to the resource library that most places have handy right in their own workplace to the Internet and related social networks that can be accessed at home, on the cell, in the car, at the office or even while sitting in the park with most electronic devices. So why must students drive themselves crazy studying for a test or exam? Young people have all kinds of undue stress thrown at them on a regular basis in real-life situations, so why make exams an added unnecessary headache?

I can almost guarantee that less than 24 hours after writing an exam, students have forgotten most if not all of the information—not only the answers to the question but the questions themselves. But I should be the last person to criticize the system, because back in high school, I was fortunate enough with my marks that I was exempt from having to write any final exams. That was important, as I was asked by classmates of various classes to write their exams for them, especially Math, English and Science. It was a very easy way to earn $40 to $50, which was a lot of money back then. Each year I would write four or five exams for others, which took no more than an hour. All I had to do was change my handwriting a touch—and, more importantly, make sure there were no teachers in the cafeteria watching over students writing the exam who would recognize me when I entered the cafeteria. As mentioned earlier, I had to do what I had to do to survive from my early teens, and at the time I never considered what the consequences could have been if I was caught.

# Express Lines 1-8

Most large food stores and department stores now have express lines, but in all honesty, what's the use? I always make sure that I am under so as not to create any confrontation with the cashier or those behind me, but more often than not I find the person in front of me has a cart full of items that doubles or even triples the posted amount. People are not so stupid that they can't count the number of items properly before proceeding to the cashier.

That's another reason your fingers can be useful, and I don't mean using the middle one. There are 10 digits total for both hands, so it doesn't take a rocket scientist to figure out if the number of items in the cart exceeds the limit. To me, it's just another act of gross ignorance or lack of respect for rules, which are in place for everyone's benefit.

If the stores don't enforce the rules, I am sure shoppers are going to keep on bending and breaking them. So who is really to blame? I tried once to talk to a shopper about the excessive groceries, and all I got was a few derogatory comments not worthy of a response—and for sure not worth the aggravation and stress at the end of a long day.

# F

French on Boxes
Frustrations of Golf

# French on Boxes

Maybe it's just me, but when looking at an item in department stores or food stores, I like to know a little about the product before I purchase it. When I do that, the majority of the time, as I look at the container, the language staring back at me is French. Why is that?

I have nothing against the French language. It's a part of my Canada, and I truly hope the French speakers don't separate from us. I just wish I could have learned to speak and understand French at an early age. As the old saying goes, "It's hard to teach an old dog new tricks."

What bothers me is the boxes on the shelves have the French version facing out; in order to read the English version, you have to turn the box at least twice. This can be tricky when boxes are stacked, and even more difficult and frustrating when the boxes are large and bulky. I am sure it is equally frustrating in Quebec if the English version faces the aisle.

Maybe it's the separatists working in Ontario and the pro-English working in Quebec who are having a little fun with us. No harm done, I guess, but it certainly is awkward at times.

# Frustrations of Golf

Why is it that when I'm playing a round of golf with friends on a beautiful day, we seem to forget about the fun we're having and start complaining about how slow the group is in front of us? It seems that we can't wait to get out and play, but once there we can't wait to get it over with.

All kidding aside, I truly enjoy being a duffer along with our regular foursome that includes Yasu, Kiran and Nam. They are real gentlemen, but even then we have all used a few not-so-nice words. I guess the saying that is used in Las Vegas can be used when playing golf: "What happens on the fairway, stays on the fairway."

I've heard it said that "golf is a game where you can get rid of your frustrations or pick up more frustration." Funny how that works!

# G

Glue Doesn't Stick to the Bottle

# Glue Doesn't Stick to the Bottle

This may seem obvious to most people, but to this simple-minded human, it seems rather strange that although glue's purpose in life is to keep things together—like paper, cardboard, wood, plastics and cloth, with which it has a good record if you use the right glue for the right product—it never sticks to its container. Why is that? The containers that hold the glue are plastic tubes or plastic containers with plastic lids or caps. I assume the glue has some sort of chemical reaction when exposed to air. Such a simple answer to a sticky topic. No pun intended!

# H

Hands on a Car Roof
Have Fun: Change Letters!
How to Spoil a Family Picnic

# Hands on a Car Roof

This boggles my mind a little bit. Whether driving through the city at 50 kilometres an hour or on the highway at 100 or 120, a driver or a passenger will have an arm out the window and the hand resting on the car roof. It's not like they are trying to hold the car roof down—unless it's just been glued to the frame and they are using their hands as a clamp until the glue is dry and the pieces are bonded together as one. Somehow I doubt that's the case.

My guess is that they are nervous and the hand on the roof is for security purposes only. Or maybe there has been an argument between the two occupants and they're afraid of having their hands slapped.

# Have Fun, Change Letters

Change, add or reverse letters here and there and see how the meaning changes. I do this sometimes when I am stuck in traffic or in a doctor's waiting room. It helps pass the time a little. A group of examples would be:

- "Lend me your ear"—change to "Lend me your car" (teen to parent)
- "Lend me your ear"—change to "Lend me your rear" (a bummer)
- "Lend me your ear"—change to "Lend me your bear" (Yogi for hire)
- From George Carlin: "Prick your finger"—change to "Finger your p****."
- This one's from me: "TGIF"—change from "Thank goodness it's Friday" to "Toes go in first" (in your shoes)

# How to Spoil a Family Picnic

Have you ever been at a beach or a park enjoying yourself, basking in the sun and reading a good book, when a family or families pick a spot directly beside you and mess up your entire setting? You know what I mean. Not only is your space being trespassed, so to speak, but if you stay, you have to put up with noisy conversations, screaming children playing around you, flying Frisbees landing near or right on you, the stench of second-hand smoke from inconsiderate smokers, BBQs with foreign smells, garbage around you, pets doing their business close to you—the list goes on.

Well, I have a surefire way of getting even. Chances are, you are going to move to another spot, so do as I have done. Right before you are ready to leave, throw a little food close to where the interlopers are and watch the fun unfold when they are all of a sudden swarmed by screeching seagulls looking for lunch. These obnoxious creatures are daring by nature, and they can be downright annoying at a picnic. It's kind of surprising how many show up so fast when a few bits of food are tossed around.

I tried it once, and it worked so well the family actually got up and vacated the area before I had a chance to set up a little further along the beach. So I went back after the birds left and enjoyed the day. It may seem a little cruel or childish to pull such a prank, but I like to think of it as survival. Another and probably better way of putting it is: I don't get mad, I get even. Being angry for so many years taught me to go an alternative route, and this is the one I chose in this instance.

**I**

Intersection Lights

# Intersection Lights

When I was growing up in the 1950s, 1960s and 1970s, it seemed that all intersections had a green light, a yellow or amber light and a red light. The process was simple. When the light turned green, you would look left, look right and proceed to walk across the intersection. When the light turned yellow or amber, there were two possibilities: 1) if you were already walking in the intersection, you would hurry up a little bit to get to the sidewalk across the road before the light turned red; and 2) if you were about to step off the curb into the intersection when the light turned yellow or amber, you would stop and wait for the light to turn green. Of course, if the light was red, you would stop in your tracks and just stay put, eagerly waiting for the light to turn green.

Today, people get confused, agitated and panic-stricken when walking, especially in downtown Toronto, where there are green lights, flashing green lights, green arrows beside green lights, four lights instead of three, signs attached right next to the lights saying no turning on red lights, horizontal lights that are read left to right instead top to bottom, signs that show streetlights (a warning for lights ahead?), multiple sets of lights at a busy intersection and so on. When a green light has a red light with an imprint of a pedestrian on the lights, does it mean pedestrians can walk at this red light?

It's crazy out there, and maybe that's the trick to surviving. Being a little crazy helps. Adding to the above confusion, I have noticed that some of the green lights change too quickly. There is hardly enough time for a normal, young, healthy person to walk briskly from one side to the other before the light turns. What about elderly people, handicapped people, young mothers with strollers? It seems that we as a society have lost touch with yet another relatively simple way of getting around and made a total mess of both walking and driving. It's no wonder we have pedestrian accidents and road rage.

# J

Just Wondering

# Just Wondering

The following are just a silly few lines to ponder as to why there is no answer:

1.  New potatoes—are old ones still being sold? If so, why aren't they cheaper?
2.  Young vegetables on restaurant menus—are old ones still being sold? If so, why aren't the elderly or adult ones being sold for less?
3.  Three-piece coffee table—does it come in three pieces? Haven't seen one of those yet.
4.  Three-piece sectional couch—does it also come in three pieces? Haven't seen one of those yet either.
5.  Why are shoelaces so long? There are never enough holes in the shoe.
6.  There seem to be extra buttons on certain shirts. Is that because of an afterthought when the shirt buttonholes were miscounted?
7.  Cars go forward, but certain rims appear to go backwards. There must be an explanation for this one.
8.  Imitation crab legs—explain this one to me, please!
9.  Legal paper—there's illegal paper?
10. James—why is his name plural?

I grew up with the humour of George Carlin, a comedian of whom you will never see the likes again. He was truly one of a kind.

# K

Kleenex and the Washer

# Kleenex and the Washer

This one is mainly for the guys in the audience, since we have to admit that we are the culprits when bits of Kleenex are found all over the freshly cleaned clothes that are pulled out of the washer. It takes such an unnecessary tedious effort to rid the clothes of all of the Kleenex bits. I've done it on more than one occasion and have had my wrist slapped for it. All it takes is a 10-second check, reaching into all of your pockets and pulling out the little bits of Kleenex, paper receipts and anything else that might turn into tiny bits in water, and you'll stay out of hot water with your significant other.

Do what I've learned to do: when you take your clothes off (pants in particular), turn them inside out, including the pockets. Besides eliminating any potential pocket passengers, I've been told it makes for a better wash, and who am I to argue? I'm lucky to find the on and off button for most appliances. I've also put a pink top in with underwear, and boy does that ever change your wardrobe in a flash.

# L

Long-Distance Calls

# Long-Distance Calls

Having Scottish blood in me causes me to be a little frugal (nice word for cheap) from time to time. I've discovered that the person making a long-distance phone call is normally the one who will end up paying the long-distance charges, so I've developed a little trick. Maybe you'd like to try it too.

Make that long-distance call. Let the phone ring two or three times and then abruptly hang up. If the person is nosy or irritated enough, he or she will phone back, and then you begin your nice long conversation. To repeat: the one who makes the call gets the bill, not the one on the receiving end. You get off "Scot" free!

# M

Mailboxes Are Not Big Enough
Men's and Women's Washrooms

# Mailboxes Are Not Big Enough

Living in different subdivisions over the years where mail gets delivered to super-boxes set up methodically every few blocks, I have become accustomed to enjoying the very short walk with my dog to retrieve my mail. On occasion, I've placed mail to be delivered in that little slot on the top left-hand side of the unit, and that is where my problem lies.

Why can't the designers of these super-boxes and the companies that make greeting cards get together to design an envelope that fits in that little opening without getting bent at the corners or folded in half to fit the slot or totally destroyed—and it still won't fit.

Most cards fit, to be honest, but on occasion certain cards are just a tad longer or a touch thicker, especially if it is a fold-out card when opened. Please help fix this little problem, as I am from the old school and refuse to use social media, texting and email to wish someone a happy birthday. It always has been by phone or by card from me and always will be.

# Men's and Women's Washrooms

Have you ever noticed that when one woman in a group makes an announcement that she has to visit the ladies' room, chances are at least one other woman or the whole group has to go as well? When that happens, no one says a word about it. Yet if a man does the same thing and more than one other man goes at the same time, people will talk about it as if a crime has been committed. Why is that? We, as men, have to go as well—although not to powder our noses as women do—and sometimes it's a simple reminder when the subject is brought to our attention.

Like most other males, I always wait until the other man returns from the little boys' room before I get up to go and do my business. Just to make sure there is no gossip.

# N

Noise in the Car

# Noise in the Car

I've been driving for about forty years now—behind the wheel of a different car every four years, more or less—and more than a dozen times I have encountered something that doesn't seem right with the car. It could be a noise somewhere: under the hood, under the seats, behind you or under the trunk. Whatever it is, it plays havoc with your ears … and with your head, because you don't have a flipping clue where the noise is coming from.

To make matters worse, trying to explain the problem to a customer-service person when you bring the vehicle in is never easy. I'm sure these workers have heard it all, including listening to customers trying to mimic the sound that caused them to be there in the first place. I can bet that sometimes they play dumb themselves in order to have the customer repeat the sound or explain the noise over and over, just to mock the unfortunate motorists to their co-workers after the customer has left. I know I would, for the grouchy ones anyway.

On top of that, when you go for a test drive with a mechanic, the noise suddenly disappears, as if nothing is wrong. That's when it gets really embarrassing. It's bad enough that you make a fool of yourself trying to explain the noise or the problem, but now you can't even get the noise to happen when someone can hear it. That's when you really get the funny looks.

It's kind of like going to the dentist. The toothache seems to have subsided or disappeared once you enter the dentist's office. On the bright side, although you will have to pay both the dentist and the car dealership a pretty penny to fix your problem, at least there is no physical pain at the repair shop. There's always a silver lining.

Outhouse

# Outhouse

Why is it called an outhouse? You don't live there unless you are a fly, slug, worm, larvae or some other form of life not related to the human species.

The closest thing I've seen to anything making a home there was a skunk and a raccoon that accidently fell down the hole into the bottom of the pit. Other than that, it's a place to visit out of necessity or when nature calls. Growing up, when we spent summers at my parents' cottage in Wasaga Beach, there were times when I had to frequent this place, day or night. A quick run to the backyard in the middle of the night was a frequent occurrence, and I say *run* because the mosquitos were big and out in large numbers.

They should use another name for this little structure, like maybe "out john" or "exterior water closet" or "waste discharge container." But not outhouse.

Oh, by the way, I mentioned the skunk because I was the lucky one who found the little critter one night when I sat down to do my business. I must have startled the white-striped son of a gun, and guess where I got sprayed? You guessed right, and I ended up sitting in a bathtub of tomato juice for a bit. A real bummer of a situation.

# P

Passport Picture Problems
Personalized Licence Plates
Pharmacists and Prescriptions
Phone Response Time
Plastic Containers and Packaging

# Passport Picture Problems

People complain about the length of time they have to wait in line while applying for a passport, the length of time it takes to process it and then about the delivery of the actual passport to their place of residence. Wake up, people!

Security is of utmost importance when it comes to travelling these days, and obviously more people are applying for passports than ever. I know that most people are certain about a proposed trip out of the country and that a passport is required, which means applying for a new one or renewing one that has expired. So why would you wait until the very last minute to obtain your passport and then go into panic mode and blame everyone involved? The real problem is the procrastinator who refused to allow enough time to complete this simple necessary act before travelling.

To those latecomers I say, instead of complaining and putting the blame on the establishment for your stress, take a look in the mirror. That's where you will find the real culprit. My only problem with passport pictures is, why you can't smile? Travel is generally a happy event, so it would be nice to have a smiling picture instead of a mug shot.

# Personalized Licence Plates

Are people so insecure that they have to advertise their name on a licence plate? To me, that's near the top of the list of things that prove without a shadow of doubt that people are vain and full of themselves.

I've seen small companies advertise with their plates, but that's for business, which means money. I've seen red poppies, which show support for our troops and veterans. I've seen provincial flowers, which show how proud we are of where we live. I've seen sports logos, which show who we like and support in sports. I've seen comical lines that may show our passion, like "time4tee." But to me, it's just plain silly to advertise your name.

Most people get respect for what they do without looking for attention or accolades. Those people are very strong—confident in who they are and what they stand for. That's what gets my attention and respect. Not the nimrods or dimwits who brag about themselves.

# Pharmacists and Prescriptions

Pharmacists never cease to amaze me. They have to deal with dozens of prescriptions a day from doctors who, for some unknown reason, use what seems to be chicken scratch or some indecipherable scribble on a piece of paper. Pharmacists have to figure out not only the prescribed drug but the proper dosage as well.

It seems that doctors have forgotten how to write or print in basic easy-to-read English. Maybe they should go back to school to learn this simple skill ... but come to think of it, it may be just as easy to text or email the prescription through their cellphones or tablets, as I am sure they are tech savvy. It seems like a simple solution—maybe too simple. Maybe not a good idea, though come to think of it, doctors don't like being told much. It's a hit to their ego most of the time, and we can't have that, right?

# Phone Response Time

Trying to get through to a government or customer-service department can try the patience, to say the least. Your wait time can be anywhere from 5 minutes to 30 minutes or more, counted down minute by minute with a recorded message as you patiently wait to talk to a live person with a real live voice. Some of the music they use while you're waiting doesn't help either.

After years of going through these frustrating phone delays, I have discovered a surefire way of speeding up the process: put something in your mouth, such as food (preferably large enough that you have to chew for a bit before it goes down your throat) or fluid (especially a hot mouthful of coffee). More often than not, that's when you'll hear someone say, "Hello, how may I help you?" You then must quickly swallow the piece of food and grimace in pain if having to swallow hot coffee—not to mention clean up the mess you made if you spat the food or coffee out of your mouth and onto your desk or floor. Try it and see what I mean.

# Plastic Containers and Packaging

Who are the geniuses or masochists who design plastic containers or plastic packaging to protect products from being tampered with or from being damaged until they arrive at the home of a consumer? The packaging must stay intact while being shipped to stores, placed on store shelves, examined by potential customers, purchased and toted home. Congratulations to them, I guess, because that clear plastic packaging sure does its job. In fact, that's the problem.

When you get home and try to open that packaging, you wind up hacking at it with a pair of scissors, an X-acto blade, a screwdriver, a kitchen knife and even a skill saw. You don't just open the packaging to get at what you bought; you totally destroy the packaging—which is another concern I have. Do you know how many funny looks you get when you have to return the item for whatever reason and it has to be brought back in the original packaging along with the original receipt? Who are they kidding?

When I return an item along with the not-so-original or highly mutilated packaging, I also show the cuts, bruises, broken fingernails and screwed-up tool I used trying to get the darn thing open. You know what? It works! I don't know if that's because they believe me or they just have pity on me, but it works. Like I say, honesty is always the best policy.

# Q

Quit Golf When ...

# Quit Golf When ...

My golfing group does not play on a regular basis. I can't speak for the rest of them, but in my opinion, we are not that good at the game. I may actually be the one holding us back by making bone-headed plays from time to time. I've thought that maybe I should quit this game and find something else to do, like jigsaw puzzles. These thoughts of quitting come to me whenever one of the following happens:

- My second or third putt is longer than my first.
- While travelling down the fairway, my entire golf bag flips out of the cart while going over a bump.
- When I get to the next hole, I realize that I left my pitching wedge somewhere on the previous hole.
- While getting into the golf cart, I smack my head on the roof of the cart.
- Divots go farther than my ball.
- I am concerned about consequences when my tee shot does not go past the ladies' tee.
- I forget to put the basket down before the driving-range balls leave the machine.
- I get home and discover I have fewer clubs than when I started the round.
- Canada Geese line up in front of your shot not worried as they seem to know that you are not going to hit the ball in a straight line.

# R

Roads Are in Bad Shape Because ...

# Roads Are in Bad Shape Because ...

I honestly believe the state of our roadways is a safety issue or a traffic-ticket deterrent. While driving in the city, there are so many potholes, bumps, depressed sewers and grooves that separate the roads that you would have to be crazy to attempt to take a bite of a sandwich or an apple without putting your tooth through your tongue or trying to take a quick sip of a hot coffee that you just picked up from Tim's or McDonald's without burning either your lip or your throat, not to mention wearing the coffee somewhere on your clothes. I've done that a couple of times and have destroyed a white shirt and tie; another time I had what looked like a miss-in the urinal or did not make it to the urinal in time stain. Embarrassing to say the least!

Now I only take a drink of coffee at a red light or in a parking spot near where I bought the coffee. Sometimes it seems best to just wait until I get out of my car and head to my office.

# S

Screwdrivers
Seagull Survey
Self-Hemming Pants
Sewers and Alignment
Single, Single
Snow on the Car
Snowflake Theory
Socks Disappearing

# Screwdrivers

I may not be the sharpest tool in the shed, and I've never pretended to say that I know it all, but I have a difficult time trying to figure out why there are so many shapes of screwdriver heads just to put a screw into an object—like Phillips and Robertson, to name two.

I know that screws have different lengths, shapes, diameters, pitches and head sizes; that they are designed and used depending on their requirements; and that every job requiring screws is unique. Still, could there not have been a simpler idea of using one type of screwdriver that could fit all screw heads? If there was, we wouldn't have to carry such an arsenal of different-shaped ones in different sizes. Maybe it's just too simple of a thought, but the stress level would be a lot lower if we didn't always have to find the right one to use. Chances are you don't have that particular shape, and now you have to go out and buy one.

# Seagull Survey

My personal favourite radio station, 680 News, mentioned in a newscast on October 2, 2006, that there were approximately 40,000 seagulls at Queens Quay waterfront. I don't know which is weirder: the fact that there were that many birds in one area crapping all over or that somebody was able to count all 40,000.

What do they do to come up with that number? Count the birds one by one, or with a clicker as they fly by? Do the birds actually line up and go through a turnstile like in the subway? Maybe they bring a signed document (signed with a quill pen of course) stating their identity. Maybe they show their bird work permit with a number. Who knows?

# Self-Hemming Pants

Why can't they come up with a unique yet simple solution for men who don't want to waste time and money paying someone to hem their pants. I have personally destroyed the bottom of my pants more than once because I didn't make the time to have a proper hem put in. I know it doesn't take much to do so, but I just felt it was an unnecessary action to take. That is, until I either noticed my pants separating or tripped over them because they were a little too long.

How about pants with strips of two-sided carpet tape or Velcro? Maybe even buttons that can adjust up and down to the right length, or a couple of horizontal rows of zippers? I am sure there has to be a solution for this. I think I will put it on my to-do list.

# Sewers and Alignment

Why is it that when driving along a nice long road where the cars go straight and you should not have to turn the steering wheel because you are going in a straight line, the street sewers are not in a straight line as well? Do they not do a survey along such a stretch of road so the sewers are in line with each other? Maybe they ran out of string so they couldn't make a straight line? It's not rocket science.

It seems you have to swerve all over the place in order to avoid these uncalculated and car-menacing sewers. It's almost similar to playing or driving in an off-road adventure, in which case you need either an ATV or four-wheel drive in order to complete your trip. Add to that constant weather variance over the years that causes the roads to move a little, lowering the sewers over time until the road looks a little like the Bermuda Triangle. The only explanation I can come up with is that the road-maintenance people, whether it be the city or private companies, must get a nice kickback from repair shops that specialize in front-end alignments.

# Single, Single

Grabbing a coffee from Tim's or McDonald's (my personal favourite) used to be easy. Walk in, step up to the counter and with a heartfelt smile and a clear voice say, "May I please have a medium regular coffee?" But to my surprise, on more than one occasion after taking my first sip of java, I have sensed that something was not right. As I took off the lid, I noticed that there was no cream, and the taste definitely told me there was no sugar. Bottom line, from now on, if it is not one of my most common places to get coffee, I always say "single, single," which means one milk and one sugar.

Speaking of my personal favourite, if I have a choice between the two, McDonald's will always win, as the people are just a little bit friendlier with slightly bigger smiles, and that's from experience. I have absolutely no issues with Tim Horton's, however, as I do not hesitate to frequent one when I am in need of a caffeine fix.

# Snow on the Car

This one is a little confusing—or maybe, just maybe, there is a reason why this happens. Maybe there is a deranged snowman out there, and for whatever reason he has a vendetta against people like me who used to like knocking them over on front lawns as a kid. The snowman could use his connections with Old Man Winter to make life difficult for people like me. At any rate, it does not matter what direction I park my car, it does not matter the velocity of snow falling, it does not matter what direction the wind is from or the amount of wind blowing: every time I get back to my car, the snow is built up on the driver's side and not the passenger side.

Do you know how difficult it is to get into the car with all that snow? There have been times when it's been easier to enter through the passenger side and slide across to the driver's seat. But even then, there's a chance of having some part of your body get bruised or battered along the way, and you still have that snow to worry about before you drive off. You can't win.

# Snowflake Theory

It's been mentioned somewhere in *National Geographic* or by a leading senior Canadian climatologist that since the beginning of time, there have been roughly 10 followed by 34 zeros snowflakes fallen, and it is virtually impossible to have two of the same shape or design. I find that hard to believe. A report by the United Nations dated October 2011 put the world's population at slightly more than 7 billion, and we all know that somewhere on this planet there is another person exactly like us. So you do the math. I know it's just a comparison of two opposites with nothing in common, but really, no two snowflakes the same? I don't think so.

# Socks Disappearing

I know I am not alone in this one. A lot of people with whom I associate with have this dilemma, but unfortunately, it's mainly men.

Almost every time my clothes are washed and hung up to dry (we don't use a dryer too often as the clothes always smell better when they're dried by the sun), there seems to be an uneven number of socks to put away. I even try to match them up before they enter the washing machine, but that doesn't really help. They still come out with at least one sock escaping into the unknown, never to be seen again. Even when there are an even number when counted, there are times when two different colours have vanished and I am now left with two missing socks and two useless socks for my feet.

The only positive is at least I now have something to use as a duster or cloth to help wipe dirt from the car. I've been told that things happen for a reason, but I would much rather buy cloths, which are cheaper than argyle socks. But at least I can say I clean with class and style.

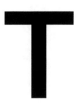

# T

Traffic Delays in Opposite Directions

# Traffic Delays in Opposite Directions

Ever noticed when driving that when there is an accident or construction that slows down traffic or brings it to a complete standstill, the traffic in the opposite direction seems to be at a slow crawl or in some cases also stopped? Why is that? There is really only one answer to that question: people are just too darn nosy.

Travelling on the 400 series highways in and around Toronto, I have been personally involved in this situation on more than enough occasions. Unless you are a police officer, fireman, paramedic or tow-truck driver, you should mind your own business and carry on with your eyes straight ahead, your hands on the wheel and your focus on where you are going. Otherwise, you could put yourself in a similar predicament to the one you are staring at. It has happened. People run into the car in front of them because of their nosiness—or, as I would say, ignorance of the road and conditions. There is another name used, and I think it is called a brain fart.

If the accident is of importance to you, catch it on the news when you get home. You always get a better view of the scene there, and without getting frustrated as well.

Speaking of frustrated, being stuck behind a road blockage due to an accident is no fun, but I have come to realize that I have no right to complain and get mad. I am just thankful that I am not part of the accident. It may be an inconvenience if a minor fender-bender, expensive if a major accident (between repair and insurance) and catastrophic if there are also injuries or a fatality.

Do as I do when this occurs and just be thankful you are not part of it. You may return home a little late, but always in one piece and in the same car. "Life is a privilege": those are four very important words, and I say them to myself when I open my eyes every morning.

Maybe I should have put this topic in the serious "Thoughts to Ponder" section rather than the lighter side, but sometimes a little sense of humour is required for certain people, especially the nosy ones who cannot keep their noses out of anyone's business. I know that I am related to a few, and it drives me nuts to listen to them at times.

# U

Underwear Must Be Clean

# Underwear Must Be Clean

This old mother's saying has been around for decades, but I wonder, do we as men have to carry a clean pair with us wherever we go? I know that it was preached to me before I left the house every day by my mother, but I always wondered if she was telling me for personal hygiene reasons or more because she would be embarrassed if she had to come to the hospital in a worst-case scenario. Mothers seem to know best when it comes to these things, but when your wife or girlfriend reminds you, it's kind of an insult to the male ego.

Although, come to think of it, there are times when standing next to someone in line you must wonder of a person who has an odour with his clothes on, *I guess his mother never talked to him growing up*. It happens more often than you'd think. That's why I always have a clean pair on every day. Come to think of it though, if I was true to my Scottish blood, I would not have to worry about any underwear at all, now would I? Just a thought!

# V

Viagra

# Viagra

What's with this little pill, and why is it so popular? I mean, it's a pill that is intended to inspire and rekindle your love life, but for what? Are men so insecure that they have to tell their friends about their love life? If they do, I bet you that they are not mentioning the little blue pill that helps them out.

Compare this to a baseball scenario. A player gets to first base via a walk, not a hit, and then gets replaced by a pinch runner named Viagra. That pinch runner manages to steal second and eventually finds his way home—commonly known as orgasm. Although the team scores, it would probably never have happened without a little help from a pinch runner and a couple of timely hits. But I guess the expression "take one for team" could apply here.

My philosophy is that things happen and don't happen for a reason, so why not let nature decide for you? There is more to life than sex, and why risk it for 15 minutes of fame? That is, if you can manage to last that long. For us older guys, there are possible side effects, starting with a heart attack. But I guess if you are going to go, it's a nice way of going out. With a bang, that is. Now that pun was intended.

# W

Water and Bottles
Weather
Why Rush From a Green Light?
Wind Two Ways
Windshield Wiper Woes
Why Three Hours Before Takeoff?

# Water and Bottles

Why is it that when water bottles, after being kept in the fridge to become colder or in the freezer to become colder faster or frozen, are left on the counter for a bit, they have water on the outside of the container? It doesn't matter if the container is plastic, glass or metal—there seems to be a film of water or drops of water on the exterior. It doesn't matter if the bottle is full or half full. It's like there is a crack somewhere in the container or a couple of pinholes that only let water out, not in. I would love for someone to give me a logical explanation for this one.

# Weather

People complain about the weather—it's too cold, too hot, too damp, too wet, too humid, too dry, too much snow, not enough snow, too much rain, not enough rain. All this complaining or worrying can be stressful, but you know what? There is nothing anyone can do about it, so just enjoy it. Look on the bright side: If it rains, it helps the flowers and vegetables grow. If it snows, it gets children and adults outside to play.

The one thing that most people do not realize is that the weather, no matter what it is, gets people talking. The more bizarre the weather gets, the more total strangers will talk to each other about it. The weather actually brings people together. Maybe it's Mother Nature's way of telling us to get along more with our fellow man. Sometimes it takes a kick in the butt to remind us to do just that.

But I guess that as humans, we must complain about something, so why not the weather? It's just human nature to complain. To tell you the truth, I get a kick out of it when I see and hear people complain about topics like the weather. It helps me have a better day.

This is not to be confused with my other item about "Weather And Conversation" as here, although similar, is more about trying to get the point across by just enjoying the moment, regardless of the weather. You cannot change the weather, so just go outside and embrace it by yourself.

# Why Rush from a Green Light?

It never ceases to amaze me the way certain drivers are determined to get a quick start when a light goes green, pounding on the gas pedal and jumping ahead of the car next to them like they're at a NASCAR or an Indy race and the green light is the signal that the race is on. I have done a survey on a few occasions while driving through city streets where intersections and lights are common, and 8 out of 10 times I will see and join those speed demons at the next red light. So why hurry?

Slow down, save a little gas and be good to the environment. Enjoy the ride instead of getting frustrated by having to put the brakes on at the next set of lights. I know it must irritate them, because occasionally I glance over to see who the maniac behind the wheel is, and let me tell you, if looks could kill, I would not be here today. If you want to make matters worse, look at them, shrug your shoulders with a questionable look on your face and smile to see how fast they give you the finger. But be careful who you do it to, as road rage has started over less than a smile.

# Wind Two Ways

As an avid daily inline skater (16 kilometres a day) after work and on the weekends up until a few years ago, I found that there was always a little mystery that I could not figure out. It's pretty simple to explain what would happen on these particular days, but my question was always why?

I would start from point A and proceed to skate on this path until I reached point B, which was approximately eight kilometres away, and then proceed back to point A. Normally it would take 60 minutes round trip, although younger and more sports-oriented people would be faster than that. Sometimes I would get lucky to have wind push me from the back, making it slightly easier and a little quicker in one direction. Unfortunately, there were days when the wind would be in my face, slowing me down a bit. It was a struggle on certain days. I thought it would be fun going back, but no! It seemed like someone had either turned the wind in the opposite direction as I was making the loop at the halfway mark to return, or someone had turned the path around so that once again, the wind was in my face. I wish someone would explain to me how it could happen so quickly.

I thought of skating backwards when this kind of weather occurred but soon realized that idea was not going to work!

# Windshield Wiper Woes

Trying to clean your vehicle in winter before heading out can be painful in itself, as you freeze your buns off clearing snow and slush from your car and particularly the windshield. I mean, it's bad enough when you get cold and wet brushing away the snow as the law requires you to do, but it's downright crazy trying to scrape the ice from your windshield, clearing the part where the snow and ice slide down the glass to where your wipers are frozen. It's virtually impossible to scrape the ice off the wiper itself without either getting frostbite or having your fingers frozen somewhere on the car—all the while knowing that somewhere down the road, there will be a piece of ice or slush that gets stuck to the wiper and ruins your visibility by smearing the windshield. On top of that, there's the freshly falling snow that builds up on the wiper and causes more problems. My only question is, "Why is it always the driver's side that messes up?" Or is it just me?

# Why Three Hours Before Takeoff?

Why do airlines make you check in three hours early for an international flight when people behind the counter themselves do not open up until an hour and a half to two hours before the flight? Am I missing something?

On two occasions, I had to catch early flights to the United States (St. Louis and Washington) when I ventured out of my comfort zone to seek employment abroad. There I was, standing in line with a whole bunch of other people waiting to check in, and the counter was closed with no one in sight. With less than two hours before flight time, everyone seemed to suddenly show up. If these people are to be professional and respected, they should lead by example, and being tardy is not going to go over well with a lot of people—including me.

Every job is important, and there are standards to live up to. When you are in the public eye, it is essential to be customer-friendly, because good customers are smart customers, and smart customers know that there are alternate carriers to use when travelling. Once we change, it's hard to get us back. At the very least, they could give us free coffee, a muffin and a newspaper while waiting. Just saying!

# Xylophone, for Example

# Xylophone, for Example

Although I have a pretty good understanding of the English language and how to use it, I find it a little confusing at times—not only for spelling, but spelling and pronunciation. Put those two together and it is a tricky language to learn.

Take xylophone, for example. Who came up with the word, spelling and pronunciation? Why not make it simple by using phonics, which simply put means spell it like it sounds or say it like its spelled. Pretty simple, I say. Don't get me going with words like elephant, sapphire, telephone and weigh.

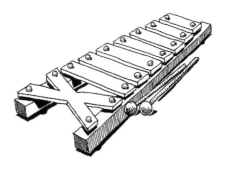

# Y

You Know You're Getting Old When ...

# You Know You're Getting Old When ...

There are probably a lot more scientific and medical terms for the signs of old age, but the following is my list of hints that you are getting old, in layman's terms. Close friends of mine will agree that a few may be from personal observation, but I am not going to admit which ones. You know you're getting old when ...

- you go to the bathroom more than four times a day.
- your bathroom trips no longer sound like Niagara Falls but more like a leisurely stream.
- while shaving, you start worrying about ear and nose hair.
- you know where the washrooms are in malls.
- you spend a lot more time in drugstores than you used to (and like it).
- you start thinking of going to church.
- while in drugstores, you start looking for Metamucil and denture cream instead of condoms and toothpaste.
- while reading the paper, you start reading the obituaries.
- you stop looking for the Sunshine Girl in the *Toronto Sun*.
- you start wearing socks with sandals.
- you bend over and have difficulty tying your shoelaces.
- like clockwork, lunch is at noon, supper is at five and bedtime is ten.
- you start thinking of senior discounts.
- your belt line gets higher.
- you button your shirt up and discover an extra button left over.
- you get excited about a sale on oatmeal and all-bran.
- you start driving with both hands on the wheel and following the speed limit.

# Z

Zebras Must Be Confused
Zippers—Why Do They Have Teeth?
Zoology 101
Zucchini

# Zebras Must Be Confused

Talk about being confused. If there is any animal in need of an animal psychologist, it has to be the zebra. Can you imagine? Not only are you prancing around trying to figure out if you are a horse, a zebra or a donkey, but you also are trying to figure out if you are black with white strips, white with black stripes or even have a touch of brown and pink. Talk about being royally confused about one's own identity! You have to admit, though, that they are beautiful, peaceful and confident creatures.

It's too bad that some people who see others as different treat them differently and unfairly at times. We as humans should accept others for who they are and not what we make them out to be. Just because there is a difference in looks, colour or belief doesn't give us the right to judge them. We are all beautiful in our own right and should be proud of who we are. I say that with sincerity, and I am not horsing around—no pun intended. Sorry about that, Mr. Zebra.

# Zippers—Why Do They Have Teeth?

Where did they come up with the word *teeth* to describe the parts of a zipper? *Zipper* is an odd name in itself, don't you think? The teeth in my mouth do not align in the same fashion as the teeth of a zipper, so again I ask, "Why are they called teeth?"

I am thinking that maybe another name would have been more suitable for a zipper—such as a hose cabinet (when opened and used during an emergency, something in a liquid form shoots out to put out some sort of a fire) or maybe even an arrest deterrent (if exposed in the wrong place, it could lead to possible confinement behind bars). This may sound silly, but let's try to keep it simple once in a while. The English language is confusing as it is.

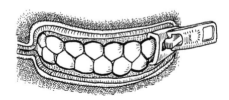

# Zoology 101

According to an article in a men's magazine dated February 2003, experiments were prepared to do some tampering with the animal kingdom to come up with a new unique species of mammal.

I think they were planning to breed an elephant with a cheetah and a porcupine with a bat as a couple of examples. If that's the thinking and the way of the scientific future, I am glad I will not be around when it happens. But then again, those morbid and sick minds must be around now in order to get the ball rolling. So it does scare me to think what they are working on. Who knows, they could be your next-door neighbours, and that's the main reason I don't let my dog out for a tinkle on her own. I just want to make sure she doesn't disappear. You never know!

# Zucchini

What is this, and where does the name come from? Who on earth came up with that name? Of course, there quite a few words that rhyme with zucchini: rotini, Lamborghini, Houdini, eenie, meenie, geography, martini, maternity, beanie and the list goes on.

English is such a unique language, but silly at the same time. It's hard enough trying to pronounce these words, but trying to spell them is a whole different ball game. (See *xylophone* a few pages back.)

# 4
# FINAL THOUGHTS

I have come to the following conclusion, and I will dare anyone to disagree with me: the Gordon name is synonymous with the word *survivor*. There is a whole lot of family to back me up on this (the McRaes and the Willkies are a couple more members of our family that come to mind). You may knock us down, but I can guarantee you that we will not only bounce right back up, but we will bounce right back up with more fight, more gusto and more determination to succeed than before you knocked us down.

This has been proven time and time again ever since I can remember. The only difference is that we don't get up with anger or animosity or self-pity or a desire to get even. We get up, reflect and learn from what happened; dust ourselves off; and become better people as well as a little wiser. That is, unless someone has hurt a family member in any shape or fashion, and then we can and probably will be your worst nightmare.

Over the years, I have learned that compassion, understanding, acceptance, love, gratitude, respect and forgiveness—not to mention a sense of humour—are the key components in helping you not only survive in today's world but also make yourself a better person. Can you imagine how great it would be if we were all wired like that? Unfortunately, that's not reality. I tell my children that you cannot change the way others think, but you can make the world a better place by being a better person. Be the type of person you want to meet.

I strive to be a better person every day. I open my eyes, as there is always room for improvement—or as my brother in-law Gord once told me, "I may not be perfect, but they don't come any better." He would say things like that with a boyish but caring smile making light of himself by quite often saying the opposite. Always encouraging with his sense of humour, yet very humble.

There are always going to be trying and difficult times in your life. My kids have bent the rules and will attest to that, but as I have mentioned, we always bounce right back up, and as human beings those challenges are given to us for a reason.

Life is a privilege and does not always have a fairy-tale ending. We sometimes need a reality check or a slap in the face, so to speak, to appreciate what we have, not what we don't have. I know I do, and I know that most of the people I associate with on a daily basis do. My circle of family, friends and co-workers give me reason to smile.

I would hope that I have shown and taught my children—Jason, Nicholas, Andrew and Jennifer—the value of being a good person, and that they understand and appreciate the importance of what I was trying to teach them. I have mentioned to people on a few occasions that although there are faults to overcome and mistakes to learn from, I can honestly say with humility and pride that every night before I close my eyes, in my mind I know that I have not hurt anybody physically, emotionally or financially, and that allows me to be at peace with myself.

Somewhere earlier in this book, I mentioned that a lot of people have put a smile on my face, and I just wanted to mention their names so as to let them know and to show off the people I have been fortunate to come across over my lifetime. There are probably a few others I have forgotten, but the following are to me the most important, as they are the ones who made me smile every time I saw them or heard their voice. They have always and continue to "make a bad day good and a good day better." To them I will simply and humbly say, "Thank you from the bottom of my heart." I just hope that I have spelled the names right but if not please accept my apologies.

## My Family

| Dorothy* (Sister) | Edward* (Brother) | George* (Brother) | Henry* (Brother) | Vera* (Sister) | Margaret* (Mother) | Adam* (Father) |
|---|---|---|---|---|---|---|
| Calvin* | Edward | George | Candy | Debbie | | |
| Gerry* | Lucy | Judy | Craig | Gord | | |
| Lindy | Maria | | Kelly | Laura | | |
| Lori | Susanna | | Scott | Tanya | | |
| Marty | | | | | | |
| Mike | | | | | | |
| Robbie* | | | | | | |

*(Deceased)

| Andrew (Son) | Jason (Son) | Jennifer (Daughter) | Nicholas (Son) |
|---|---|---|---|
| | Bailea Doreen Angel (granddaughter) | | Benjamin Johannes (grandson) |
| | Brooklyn Chelsea Sunshine (granddaughter) | | Jack Alexander (grandson) |
| | | | Sadie Elizabeth Rose (granddaughter) |

## Personal Favourites

- Jomar
- Marybel (without her patience, guidance, understanding and caring personality, I would probably be six feet under pushing up daisies by now)
- Yasu
- Kwan

**CPS Co.**
Gary
Gibson
Mike

**Ontario Formwork**
Bob
Karl
Sam

**Avenue Structures**
Carmine
Corrado
Emilio
Ken
Tony
Vic

**A.W. Hooker**
Joe

**Hardrock Forming**
(my adopted family)
Aldo
Alice
Alissa
Antonietta
Chad
Chris
Connie
Dan
Danko
Dino
Ela
Elena
Ernesto
Halyna
Jason

Keith (retired but still fondly remembered for his words of wisdom and sense of humour)
Luciano
Marco
Mark
Michael
Mirka
Nola
Paul
Piero

**Italform**
Cristina
Italo
Marco
Sandro
Silvia

**Black's Camera** (Woodbridge)
Sean

**Chrysler Dealership** (Rexdale)
Ron

**Tim Horton's** (Highway 7 and Weston–Vaughan)
John and the entire staff

**McDonald's** (Bolton)
Entire staff

**J's Café** (formerly Coffee Time—Highway 7 and Martin Grove)
Jay

**Hallmark Cards** (Woodbridge)
Jenny and the entire staff

**Sports Collectibles** (Etobicoke)
Cam
Michael

**Westmore Auto** (Etobicoke)
Onur

**Financial Institution** (Brampton)
Zoran

**Verona Florist** (Woodbridge)
Joe and Dora

**IPC Investment Corp**
(Mississauga)
Nancy

**Caritas**
Father John

**Neighbours**
Juan and Carmen (Etobicoke)
Harjinders (Brampton)

Printed in the United States
By Bookmasters